EAST ANGLIA
& NORTH THAMES

EXPLORING WOODLAND

WOODLAND
TRUST

EAST ANGLIA
& NORTH THAMES

Edited by Graham Blight

FRANCES LINCOLN LIMITED
PUBLISHERS

Acknowledgements

Introduction by Archie Miles
Site entries written by Sheila Ashton
Researched by Janet Watt
Edited by Graham Blight
Maps by Linda M Dawes, Belvoir Cartographics & Design
Regional maps created using Maps in Minutes data ©MAPS IN MINUTES™/
Collins Bartholomews 2007
Site maps © Woodland Trust

Photographic acknowledgements

Archie Miles: 8, 13, 81; Brian Gadsby/Science Photo Library: 67;
Bjorn Svensson/Science Photo Library: 70; Forestry Commission: 33
Foto 45: 19, 26, 27, 29, 46, 55, 86, 92, 95, 108; Sandra Lousada: 77
WTPL: 1 (Nicholas Spurling), 2 (Nicholas Spurling), 11 (Andrew Butler), 14 (Dave
King), 21, 31(Mike Brown), 34 (Dick Todd), 43 (M. Taylor), 45 (Pete Holmes), 49, 50
(Keith Huggett), 52 (Dave King), 60 (Keith Huggett), 62 (Andrew Butler), 65, 69
(Nicholas Spurling), 72 (Helen Parr), 79 (David Lund), 84 (Neil Sinden), 85 (Helen
Parr), 88 (Bob MacDonald), 90 (Bob MacDonald), 100 (Libby Owen), 101 (Archie
Miles), 103 (Steven Kind), 104 (Uta Read), 115 (Keith Huggett)

Frances Lincoln Ltd
4 Torriano Mews
Torriano Avenue
London NW5 2RZ
www.franceslincoln.com

East Anglia & North Thames
Copyright © Frances Lincoln 2008
Text © Woodland Trust 2008
Maps © see above

First Frances Lincoln edition: 2008

A catalogue record for this book is available
from the British Library.

ISBN 978-0-7112-2670-8

Printed and bound in Singapore
The paper used in this book was sourced from
sustainable forests, managed according to FSC
(Forest Stewardship Council) guidelines.

1 2 3 4 5 6 7 8 9

Half title page Berries at Tring Park

Title page Penn Wood

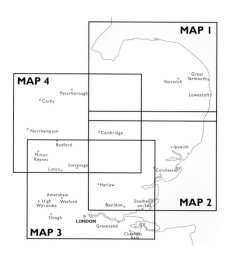

Contents

How to use this guide

Covering a region that encompasses East Anglia and the north Thames, this book is divided into four areas represented by key maps on pages 16–17, 36–37, 58–59 and 98–99. The tree symbols on these maps denote the location of each wood. In the pages following the key maps, the sites nearest one another are described together (wherever practical) to make planning a day out as rewarding as possible.

For each site entry the name of the nearest town/village is given, followed by road directions and the grid reference of the site entrance. The area of the site (in hectares followed by acres) is given together with the official status of the site where appropriate and the owner, body or organisation responsible for maintaining the site. Symbols are used to denote information about the site and its facilities as explained in the next column.

Type of wood

Mainly broadleaved woodland

Mainly coniferous woodland

Mixed woodland

Car park

Parking on site

Parking nearby

Parking difficult to find

Official status

Area of Outstanding Natural Beauty

AONB

Site of Special Scientific Interest SSSI

Site facilities

Sign at entry

Information board

One or more paths suitable for
  wheelchair users

Dogs allowed under supervision

Waymarked trail

Toilet

Picnic area

Entrance/car park charge

Refreshments on site

East Anglia & North Thames

Hayley Wood

A fine spring morning in Hayley Wood, to the southwest of Cambridge, is always an uplifting experience. Find an open glade where coppicing has taken place in recent years, sit down with a flask of tea, put your back against a fine straight oak, and soak up the refreshment, not just of the tea, but also the colourful patchwork of springtime flowers bursting forth across the woodland floor. A bluebell haze, dotted with white anemones, violets and the gently nodding sulphur-yellow stars of oxlips add to the floral show. Seemingly a cross between primrose and cowslip (a hybrid of similar appearance does exist) this is actually a rare species in its own right. Now confined to about 100 woods in Suffolk, Essex and Cambridgeshire this beautiful little flower is an indicator of ancient woodland.

Take a stroll around Hayley Wood and you'll find evidence of its former custodians, for a remarkably well-preserved woodbank, probably as old as the wood itself, reminds you of the perennial need to protect woodland from grazing beasts. Sit quietly and who knows you may be lucky enough to hear the sweet song of nightingales.

The very existence of Hayley Wood is documented as far back as the 11th century, and it was clearly a regularly managed woodland producing both timber and coppice wood for a variety of owners down the centuries. Principally oak standards with field maple, ash and hazel coppice, traditional management was renewed in 1962 when the local Wildlife Trust gained ownership of the wood. Sometimes this has proved an uphill battle; witness the deer fences around the wood (some things never change). Fallow deer have a great liking for trees and flowers and most especially, so it would seem, for oxlips.

As a region it would be difficult to find one containing greater contrasts of woodland cover than East Anglia. To the west lie the counties of Bedfordshire and Hertfordshire, which have long supported dense populations and seen erosion of their woodland in favour of agricultural improvement. Running north to south through the middle of the region lie the counties of Cambridgeshire and Essex, and these, along with the western parts of Suffolk, contain some of the finest and best-documented ancient woodland in the whole of Britain. Farther east and heavy clays give way to light sandy soils, more widely planted with conifers, although there are several remarkable enclaves of ancient oaks usually to be found in old parklands.

Bedfordshire lost a large proportion of its ancient woodland during the medieval period when agricultural demands saw it pinned back to the less fertile areas such as the greensand ridge around Woburn. Some woods were under the ownership of abbeys or priories, who derived income from rents or wood sales, whilst others were incorporated into deer parks. Woods reached their commercial peak during the 19th century when the demand for coppice wood was at its height, but by the end of the century, as coal eclipsed wood, their vibrancy declined as many fell out of regular management. Bramingham Wood is one of the most interesting in the county, particularly given its urban location, less than three miles from Luton and surrounded by housing. In this little oasis you can wander through primroses, bluebells and wood anemones, watch nuthatches and tree creepers going about their business or try to spy frogs and smooth newts in the two ponds. In the autumn go on a fungi foray and see if you can identify some of the national rarities which this wood supports.

Heading eastwards, Cambridgeshire is also a county largely given over to agriculture, yet it still retains a scattering of small woods (less than one per cent of the land). Many of the county's woods have been particularly well researched, since a remarkable collection of early documents exist which detail their ownership, management and trade. Just over the border lies Bedford Purlieus, famed for a detailed study made in 1975 which identified almost 400 vascular plant species (a record in one wood). What on earth is a purlieu? It's a piece of private land next to a forest, often released from forest laws.

Like Hayley Wood, nearby Gamlingay is also an oak, ash, maple and hazel wood, hiding all manner of ancient earthworks, woodbanks and ditches. If you have a yearning to see some elms, or what's left of them, get yourself to Knapwell, but don't be depressed by the apparent decline of Overhall Grove. The rotting carcasses of once handsome elms take on the appearance of an elephants' graveyard – Dutch elm disease detritus – but hold hard, check the undergrowth carefully and you'll find young suckers thrusting up from the root systems. The oak and ash will fair a little better while the elm overcomes the attentions of the little bark beetles and the fungus they import. Evolutionary genetics or resistance will ensure that big elms will make it back to the landscape some day, meanwhile the dead wood makes grand mansions for bugs of all kinds and bat roosts, as well as feeding grounds and nesting sites for birds. The racket of a woodpecker hammering is never far away here.

The woods of West Suffolk closely resemble those of Cambridgeshire and one of the jewels in Suffolk's crown is

Penn Wood

Bradfield Woods, near Bury St Edmunds, actually comprising two adjoining woods of Felshamhall and Monkspark. The latter was once a deer park whilst the former has been a coppice wood since at least 1252. Bradfield is a species-rich woodland in every way, but this is not just a beautiful place, it is also a working wood, and it's this ongoing activity which has helped to maintain the biodiversity. Coppice wood is still extracted for making implements such as rakes and brooms, hurdles, turnery, thatching spars, stakes and posts, as well as fuel wood. A little to the east, beyond Stowmarket, lies Priestley Wood. This is another fine example of one of those wonderful remnants of ancient woodland which contains not only giant ash and field maple coppice stools, but also the more unusual hornbeam and small-leaved lime, two trees which become more apparent as you head south into Essex. Wild pear, something of a native rarity and a good ancient woodland indicator grows here, but beware if you find any of the tiny fruits in the autumn as they are mouth-wrenchingly sour.

Although the whole of Essex was Royal Forest under the rule of King John, this was only in the old legal sense of forest, meaning a reserve for deer and not necessarily covered by trees. Certainly a large proportion was given over to woodland and fortunately some splendid tracts of that physical forest still survive to this day, manifesting as some of the most extensive areas of woodland in eastern England.

Epping Forest, the largest public open space in the London area, has over 6,000 acres for Londoners (and everyone else besides) to enjoy. However, don't ever take all those magnificent oaks, beeches and hornbeams for granted, for if it hadn't been for a great uprising of public indignation in 1878 the forest might easily have been lost as a public amenity. The locals petitioned the government of the day in the wake of numerous private landowners quietly partitioning off parts of the forest, and thus eroding commoners' rights and public access. Their concerns were addressed when an Act of Parliament was passed which entrusted the care of the Forest to the Corporation of the City of London. Until recent years time stood still for the trees of Epping. Victorian pollards became hugely

Epping Forest

overgrown – part of the forest's heritage hung in the balance – vulnerable to either natural decay and demise or a cruel gust of wind. In recent times brave management by the Epping foresters has seen a reintroduction of a pollarding regime. Take a look and see what the forest might have looked like 150 years ago and more.

Hornbeam is a very distinctive feature of many Essex woods, usually as pollards or coppice stools. Occasionally mistaken for beech, its defining characteristics are a more elongated tooth-edged leaf and a grey fluted trunk. Hornbeam timber is the hardest of all native broadleaf species and, although it was once used for such purposes as windmill cogs, its main use seems to have been for fuel wood.

Hatfield Forest, famed as one of the finest examples of a wooded forest typical of the Middle Ages, contains many different variations of the hornbeam. Dense compartments of coppiced trees, which would once have been carefully guarded from livestock, are interspersed with open plains of wood pasture, dotted

Hillhouse Wood

with pollard trees. Some of these pollard hornbeams are outgrown shock-headed trees, whilst others are magical decrepit veterans sometimes split down the middle so that you can walk right through the tree! Much like Epping, there is also a new pollarding regime in action here.

Swing north to the county of Norfolk and a region of great contrasts emerges. The southwest part of the county, with its lighter sandy soils, contains the second largest forest in England (Kielder, in Northumberland, being the largest). Thetford Forest covers 50,000 acres of Breckland, and is predominantly a forest of pines – initially Scots pine, but latterly Corsican pine being preferred by the foresters – and there's plenty of heathland. If you're lucky this could be the place to see red squirrels, who live amidst the Scots pine stands, but you'll have to be cautious as they are nothing like as bold as their grey American cousins. The forest is a brilliant open space for families, with play areas for children and miles and miles of trails for belting around on bikes.

If the endless conifer belts do not inspire you, then head north and seek out some of the glorious woods associated with old ancestral parkland. Family fun is to be found at Wolterton Park, where there's an adventure playground and an orienteering course or, if you find even the thought of that a bit too exhausting, simply take a saunter along the network of well-laid-out paths and soak up the mixture of natural woodland and 300 years of tree planting by successive owners. There are some great possibilities for bird lovers here; goldcrests and crossbills in the larch and pine stands, breeding herons and, if you're really lucky, a sighting of ospreys on the fishing lake in autumn. Blickling Woods and Felbrigg Great Wood have a more sedate air about them – the former particularly notable for its fine beeches, whilst huge old oaks and sweet chestnuts feature at the latter.

Taken as a whole East Anglia is by no means a heavily wooded region, but what is on offer is of remarkable historical and biological significance. Some of these pockets of woodland are virtual time capsules of landscape and habitat which have mostly been swept away over the last 1,000 years. Pick up on the ancient aspects of these sites, compare them to other woods you know which might not immediately seem so interesting, and it will give you an amazing insight into why these woods are so very special.

Understanding and appreciating woodland can really make a difference. Bradfield Woods in Suffolk were under serious threat of clear felling in the 1960s, but because the local populace cherished and understood the importance of these woods, they made a stand to save them and were successful. This may not be the appropriate platform to rant from the soap box, but if you are passionate about woods be assured that you have the potential to make a difference.

Where you choose to go and what you want to see is down to you, and this book helps you make an informed decision. Most of the sites are managed to a greater or lesser degree, which means that rather than trying to dive into some tangled thicket, you're assured of good access.

ARCHIE MILES

MAP 1

N

10 miles
10 km

Old
Wood *p21* **West Runton &**
Sheringham **Beeston Regis Heath** *p22*
Sheringham **Cromer**
Park *p20* **Pretty** **Felbrigg Great Wood** *p23*
Corner
t Country **Wood** *p22*
ark *p20* North
Walsham
Wolterton
Mannington **Park** *p24* **Bacton Wood** *p24*
Woods *p25* Aylsham
Blickling Hall *p26*
Foxley
Wood *p28*
Hevingham
Park *p30*
A1062
A1151
Hockering A149
Wood *p27*
A47 Caister-on-Sea
reham *The*
Snakeshill A47
Wood *p30* **Norwich** **Great Yarmouth**
A47
Broads
Wymondham
A146
A143 A12
Sisland Carr *p35*
Attleborough **Lowestoft**
Three Gates
Farm *p35*
A140 **Tyrrel's**
Wood *p34* A146
Bungay Beccles
A143
A144 A145 A12
6
Diss
A143
Halesworth
Eye **MAP 2 ▼**(see p36) Southwold

17

MAP 1

Sandringham Country Park

Dersingham

On the B1440. (TF690287)
243ha (601acres)
Sandringham Estate

A walk through the woodland of Sandringham Country Park is well worth it – you might find yourself rewarded with the glimpse of a deer, squirrel, or jay.

Easy car parking and well-laid paths provide good access to woodland that is dominated by conifers and with a few broadleaves breaking the pattern. Some of the trees have been left to grow old gracefully and just a short walk from the car park you can find some fine examples of majestic-looking pines.

Popular at weekends and during the summer, the wood is largely used only by local people on weekdays so this would be a good time for a tranquil walk along one of the waymarked trails.

The park itself is well laid out and a great place to take children, with an adventure playground to keep them amused. Tractor and trailer tours of the country park are provided between April and October.

Reffley Wood

King's Lynn

Reffley Wood lies just to the east of King s Lynn and adjoins, at its southern end, the A149 King s Lynn by-pass. (TF657223)
53ha (131acres)
Woodland Trust

Reffley Wood is gradually returning to its ancient roots.

At present dominated by Scots and Corsican pine and Douglas fir, a restoration programme will re-establish broadleaved woodland, remnants of which can still be found, including a hazel and hawthorn understorey.

In the northeast corner is a row of veteran oaks, which once marked the parish boundary, and red oaks can be seen at the entrance.

Many flowers associated with ancient woodland thrive along the wide rides, including bluebells, primroses and wild garlic.

Reffley Wood

Generally a flat site, some paths stay dry throughout the year while others can become particularly wet in winter. Bear in mind that sections of the wood may be closed for management work at certain times.

MAP 1

Holt Country Park
Holt
B1149 between Holt and
Edgefield. (TG082376)
42ha (104acres)
North Norfolk District Council

Holt Country Park is a good
spot to take children for a fun
day out as it boasts both an
adventure playground and
wayfaring course – a family
version of orienteering.

Originally planted at the end
of the 19th century, the wood
was replanted with conifers after
World War II. Though it's
dominated today by conifers

you can see birch, oak, beech
and sweet chestnut regenerating.

Visit at dusk and there's a
good chance of spotting red,
roe and muntjac deer which
inhabit the woodland. A spring
visit will bring the reward of
primroses and meadow
saxifrage in bloom.

The pond is popular with
visitors as close by is a tall
timber observation tower – not
for the faint-hearted as you can
see down through the slats, so
a good head for heights is
needed. For those who make
it to the top there's a
wonderful view across the
heath and birch woodland that
lies to the east.

Sheringham Park
Sheringham
3km (2 miles) southwest of
Sheringham, access for cars off
A148 Cromer to Holt road.
(TG139412)
116ha (286acres)
National Trust

Landscaped by Humphry
Repton, Sheringham Park
features a woodland garden
with rhododendron and azaleas

that look spectacular between
May and June – great views
from a special observation
tower near the car park.

There's a raised walkway
providing some fantastic
viewpoints – you can look right
over the park to the coast.
While ideal for less able visitors,
the boardwalk does come to an
abrupt halt. Steps lead down
into the woodland, which has
some large oaks and conifers,
and follows through to the
parkland where there is an

impressive stand of beech trees.

The North Norfolk Grand Tour combines a steam train journey on the North Norfolk line with a walk between Weybourne Heath and Sheringham Park. Alternatively you can take a five-mile waymarked route from the car park which leads to the coast.

Old Wood
Sheringham

Part of a larger area of continuous woodland on higher ground at the southern edge of Sheringham, adjoining the Holt Road (A148). Car park at southwest corner of woodland. (TG160412)
23ha (57acres) AONB
Woodland Trust

Though Old Wood is currently mainly Corsican pine and Douglas fir, a conservation programme is gradually converting much of the site back to broadleaf wood and heathland.

It is hoped the heathland will eventually become one of North Norfolk's key conservation habitats – already home to adders and slow-worms.

Visitors should consider 'twinning' Old Wood with Pretty Corner Wood next to it (see next entry). There's a good contrast between the coniferous and broadleaved woodland areas, though both are now being managed for conservation.

Surfaced and mainly dry paths help visitors explore this sloping site, providing access to higher parts without having to endure long, steep gradients.

At the southern end is one of the highest points in Norfolk with splendid views across the wood to Sheringham and the sea beyond.

Old Wood

MAP 1

Pretty Corner Wood
Sheringham

From A148 take A1082 towards
Sheringham. Turn right at sign for
Pretty Corner tea gardens car
park. Car park on left. (TG153412)
29ha (72acres) AONB

North Norfolk District Council

There are some attractive trees
in this mixed wood of birch,
oak, sweet chestnut and pine
and these provide a dramatic
contrast to the neighbouring
conifers of Old Wood (see
previous entry). Healthy
young trees are popping up
everywhere, suggesting that
this aptly named wood has a
bright future.

Just five minutes walk from
the southern car park you'll
reach one of the wood's most
popular features – a house,
cosily surrounded by trees
making the most of its location
by providing a tearoom offering
refreshments to visitors.

While paths are largely well
drained some are steep but
you'll find welcoming benches
strategically placed.

West Runton & Beeston Regis Heath
Cromer or Sheringham

A148 between Cromer and Holt.
(TG184414)
46ha (113acres)

National Trust

Breathtaking views and a
fascinating history make
compelling reasons to visit
West Runton and Beeston
Regis Heath.

Set near the highest part in
Norfolk, it offers some
wonderful coastal views.

Earthworks nearby, known as
the Roman Camp, are
probably where the Romans
had a lookout. Shallow pits
mark sites where iron ore was
smelted before and during the
Middle Ages.

The woodland includes
sweet chestnut, oak, beech,
birch, rowan, Scots pine,
sycamore and holly. In the
early 20th century heather and
bracken covered much of the
area. When birch declined due
to sheep grazing, rowan and
Scots pine invaded.

Sensitive management is
maintaining a varied wildlife

habitat. All three species of woodpecker live here along with wood warblers, tree pipits and nightjar. There are also foxes, roe and muntjac deer.

You might also spot purple hairstreak, holly blue, grayling and gatekeeper butterflies. Adders live in the heather and there are common lizards and slow-worms too.

Felbrigg Great Wood
Cromer

Near Felbrigg village, 2.5km (1.5 miles) southwest of Cromer; entrance off B1436, signposted from A148 and A140. Follow brown National Trust signs. (TG195394)
132ha (327acres) SSSI
National Trust

It's easy to be impressed even before alighting from your car on a visit to Felbrigg Great Wood. Just driving through the deer park to the car park evokes a real sense of space and history.

There are oaks and chestnuts, some having grown into fine old trees, with majestic form and shape. Those that suffered in storms have become gnarled and full of character. Routes are well waymarked and the facilities are good.

The woodland walk takes you through an area that has been grazed in the past. Contrast the mature trees set in open grassland with the dense areas of birch and dark coniferous plantations.

A programme of planting and grazing is aiming to restore the woodland pasture.

MAP 1

Bacton Wood
North Walsham

From North Walsham take B1150
towards Keswick. Turn right
towards Honing. Car park on right
after Witton Hall. (TG318312)
113ha (279acres)
Forestry Commission

Believed to have had tree cover
since Saxon times, the site was
felled and replanted between
1956 and 1971, largely with
Scots and Corsican pine,
western hemlock and
Douglas fir. In one area,
dominated by larch, look for
goldcrests and warblers.

Of the original wood two
magnificent sessile oaks,
believed to be over 200 years
old, have survived – see
information board for
locations.

Today the plantation is
managed with a mix of
recreation, nature conservation,
commercial interests,
sustainability and landscape in
mind. Thinning has opened up
some areas and the rides
widened where visitors can
enjoy watching butterflies
in summer.

There is a permanent
orienteering course with map
and clear waymarked routes
throughout.

Wolterton Park
Aylsham

Signposted with brown tourist
signs from A140 Norwich to
Cromer road. (TG165317)
30ha (74acres)
Lord Walpole

The hall and grounds of
attractive Wolterton Park date
back to the 1720s when
Thomas Ripley designed them
for Horatio Walpole, brother of

Britain's first prime minister,
Sir Robert Walpole.

In 1990 it was inherited by
the present Lord Walpole, who
launched a programme of
planting and conservation
including organic grazing by
Jacob sheep.

Sweet chestnuts survive from
an avenue near the stables
planted in the 1720s, and there
are London plane and lime
along with conifers that were
planted in the 1820s. You'll
encounter some lovely big

beech trees on the approach to the hall and car park.

The park has an orienteering course, adventure playground, a spinney with some large oaks, and a fishing lake where osprey can be seen in autumn. Other park inhabitants include barn owls, kestrels, doves, sparrowhawks and in the Scots pine and larch, goldcrest and crossbills. Herons breed each year in the upper branches of larch and cormorants live on the island in the lake.

Mannington Woods
Aylsham

From A140 go through Aylsham and follow brown tourist signs to Blickling. From Blickling follow brown tourist signs to Mannington. (TG142321)
40ha (99acres)
Lord Walpole

Top of your 'must see' list on a visit to Mannington Wood is the arboretum. Don't expect a collection of exotic species as this arboretum has been laid out and planted entirely with native trees – all labelled, so excellent for learning tree identification. Lord Walpole, who took over the site in 1986, wanted to present all native broadleaf and evergreen species in appropriate settings.

The site is well laid out and interpreted with meadows, follies, woodland and a garden renowned for its roses.

In Mossymere, an ancient woodland site, you will find Scots pine and larch planted in the 1950s growing alongside oak, sweet chestnut and hazel. Look out for red, roe and muntjac deer, displays of bluebells, wood anemone and early purple orchid flowers, white admiral and purple hairstreak butterflies.

There is also a meadow with a boardwalk and wood pasture with large, 100-year-old horse chestnuts. When you reach an area of coppiced oak, birch, hazel, alder, willow and rowan you might be lucky enough to hear the song of nightingales or spot a tawny owl.

MAP 1

Blickling Hall
Aylsham

2.5km (1.5 miles) northwest of
Aylsham on B1354. Signposted off
A140 Norwich to Cromer Road.
Follow brown National Trust signs.
(TG176285)
86ha (213acres)
National Trust

There is a good day out to be
had at Blickling Hall –
particularly if you have
children who enjoy places to
run and explore.

The estate boasts some very
large trees, including oak,
chestnut, beech and pine and,
within Great Wood, you will
find a spectacular collection of
beech trees hugging the
hillside. To reach these either
use the car park to the
northwest of the estate which
faces them or follow the
estate walk.

The clear, open space
beneath the beech makes a
great play area for children and
a lovely place to kick up
colourful leaves in autumn.

Paths are well laid out and
clearly waymarked making it
easy to explore. There are good
views of the nearby tower and
other woodland on the estate
which is mixed broadleaves
and conifers.

Blickling Hall

Hockering Wood

Hockering Wood
East Dareham

Follow A47 to Hockering and then take Heath Road out of village. After 400m take first left and wood entrance on left. (TG072150)
90ha (222acres) SSSI

Mr M Hutton

Quite neglected until the mid-1950s, when it was acquired by the Hutton family, Hockering Wood has an interesting history.

Used for bomb storage by the RAF during World War I, much of the timber was felled in the 1920s, leaving a scattering of oak, beech, larch, and pine. But in the late 1950s it was replanted with larch, Douglas fir, western red cedar, red oak and sweet chestnut. There is a fine group of 70-year-old small-leaved limes.

More recently the wood has been managed for conservation and ash and hazel have been reintroduced, while thinning of conifers and broadleaves has provided some light relief – and opened up views of some stately oaks.

In spring, visitors can enjoy wonderful displays of primroses, bluebells, wood anemone, early-purple orchid and lily-of-the-valley.

MAP 1

Foxley Wood
Fakenham or Aylsham
On A1067 Fakenham road take right turn to Foxley. Entrance is
800m (0.5 mile) on right past first house out of village. (TG049229)
180ha (445acres)
Norfolk Wildlife Trust

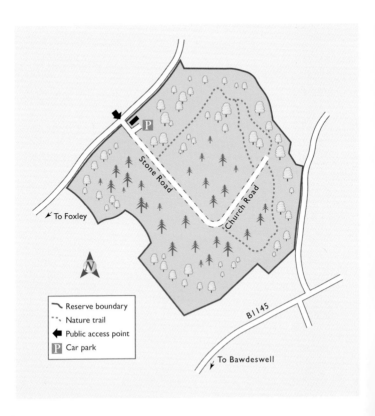

To Foxley

Stone Road

Church Road

N

B1145

To Bawdeswell

Reserve boundary
Nature trail
Public access point
P Car park

Foxley Wood

Norfolk's largest remaining semi-natural ancient woodland is the 6,000-year-old Foxley Wood, a well-managed, if muddy, site that's rich in flora and wildlife.

The wood was neglected in the 20th century, as is evident from the oak and hazel coppiced areas and sections planted with conifers during the 1960s.

However, Norfolk Wildlife Trust is re-establishing traditional coppice methods as part of an active management programme that includes thinning, pollarding, removal of conifers, restoration of rides and creation of new waymarked access tracks.

The wood's ancient status is confirmed by the sight of the rare small-leaved lime, Midland hawthorn and wild service trees.

A walk up the main ride offers a striking contrast between the open oak and coppiced trees to your left and the dark, dense conifers to the right.

The rides are rich in flora, including bog stitchwort, bugle, tufted hair-grass, common spotted and greater butterfly orchid, dog's mercury, herb-paris, bluebells, primroses and violets.

Look out for white admiral, comma and speckled wood butterflies. You might also spot a barn owl, goldfinch or lesser spotted woodpecker.

There is a circular path around the site with some helpful interpretation boards. While the main track is surfaced, boots are a good idea for your visit.

29

MAP 1

Hevingham Park
Aylsham

A140 south of Hevingham village.
(TG205206)
91ha (225acres)
Forestry Commission

This mixed plantation of Scots pine, oak, Corsican pine, larch, poplar, alder, poplar and sycamore was planted over a 20-year period, beginning in the late 1940s.

The grid-like pattern of rides means you can find your way about this surprisingly peaceful and pleasant wood, despite a lack of waymarkings, information board or leaflet.

The wood has a tendency to become very wet underfoot after heavy rains, particularly in the eastern part, although the paths appear to remain largely accessible.

You could combine your visit with nearby Blickling Hall, Hockering Wood or Foxley Wood – all featured with separate entries in this guide. Swannington Manor Gardens are also worth a look.

Snakeshill Wood
Old Costessey

Take A1067 from Norwich to Old Costessey. Go through village, past public house and park just past second turning on left.
(TG158119)
7ha (17acres)
Woodland Trust

Situated on a steep ridge overlooking Old Costessey, Snakeshill is a prominent feature of the local landscape and enjoyed by local people for its variety of oak, hornbeam, wild cherry, chestnut, beech and sycamore.

Because the ridge has just a thin layer of light soil over gravel, the wood is well drained so paths remain relatively dry throughout the year. Since acquiring the site in 1995, the Woodland Trust has extended the path network so visitors can enjoy a circular route.

From the main entrance at the eastern end, steps ascend the steep slope to join a wide path that follows the top of the ridge. On its way this route crosses a sunken track, goes through a section of rhododendron and beside rough grassland where pigs were once kept.

To the south you may glimpse the old hall and its gardens behind a high brick wall, and Costessey Park golf course beyond.

Wayland Wood
Watton

Take A1075 signposted to Thetford from Watton. Wood on left after caravan site. (TL924995)
117ha (289acres)
Norfolk Wildlife Trust

Wayland is a delightful, sensitively managed ancient woodland where the reintroduction of coppicing is already producing results.

The site includes oak, ash, beech and hazel trees and coppicing has opened up space around some of the larger trees, revealing fine old oaks.

Waymarker posts lead you on a circular route around the wood and there is also a clear ride around the site. In spring a variety of flowers add their colour including early purple orchids, yellow Star-of-Bethlehem, primrose, bluebells and wood anemone. The flowering bird cherry in spring is particularly lovely.

Bluebells adding their spring colour

MAP 1

Thetford Forest Park

Brandon

High Lodge visitor centre signed from B1107 Brandon to Thetford road.
(TL811851)
18,800ha (46,400acres) SSSI

Forestry Commission

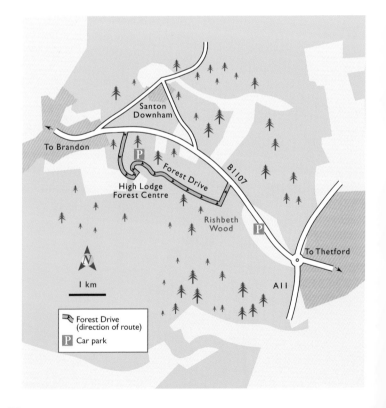

Britain's largest lowland pine forest, Thetford Forest Park is a great place for a family day out – and one of those increasingly rare places in England where it's still possible to spot the red squirrel.

First planted in 1922, the woodland has evolved into a thriving site of timber production. In the early days Scots pine dominated and is retained today as a habitat for red squirrels. The dominant tree now is the Corsican pine.

That's not to say the woodland is all pines – there are also areas of broadleaved trees and open heathland too.

One of the site's strongest points is its suitability for younger visitors and a family tour can easily stretch to an entire day, because of the ample recreation facilities and a year-round events programme.

The best place to head if you have young children is High Lodge which is a stone's throw from one of the 15 car parks and equipped with shop, toilets, café, picnic tables and play areas. Nearby is a squirrel's maze as well as giant play structures. More adventurous visitors can cycle – bike hire is available – along a series of three good trails and even explore a number of bomb craters along the way. There's a small hide at the end of one of the trails, providing a good vantage point for spotting muntjac, roe, fallow and red deer. Closer to the centre is a bat hibernaculum.

Thetford Forest Park

MAP 1

Brownies in Tyrrel's Wood

Tyrrel's Wood
Harleston or Hardwick

East of A140 Norwich to Ipswich
road, on Wood Lane. Car park at
southern end of wood.
(TM205896)
17ha (42acres) SSSI

Woodland Trust

Quiet and off the beaten
track, Tyrrel's Wood is a
welcome spot for visitors and
wildlife alike.

At the centre is an ancient
woodland site, named Boscus
de Grischave in records dating
back to 1251, and believed to
have been around since the Ice
Age – the presence of bluebells
and wood melick indicate this.
It has been designated Site of
Special Scientific Interest
(SSSI) because of the immense
variety of woodland packed
into such a small area.

Paths wind through dense
undergrowth, emerging in
open areas that boast big oak
trees. A circular route around
the site can be enjoyed and,
despite no waymarkings or
information board, is relatively
easy to follow.

A plantation was created
here in the 1830s but the
continued presence of old oak
and hornbeam pollards and
woodbanks are evidence of a
much longer history.

Sisland Carr
Norwich

From A146 take turning to Sisland (opposite turn to Loddon). Take first right and first right again along track, which leads to wood. (TM345993)

12ha (29acres)

Woodland Trust

Work is in hand to reduce the number of conifers at Sisland Carr and replace these with broadleaved trees.

Damage wreaked by the storms of 1987 prompted replanting, and young native broadleaf species are becoming well established.

The combination makes for a pleasant walk, offering a variety of woodland from close dense conifer blocks where pine needles cushion the floor, to sections where coppicing and tree-thinning has been taking place.

Easy-to-follow paths lead around the site, passing a grazed meadow which provides another good habitat for wildlife.

Three Gates Farm
Beccles

From A143 take road to Aldeby. Access to wood from Rectory Road. Woodland Trust sign visible from road. (TM456936)

4ha (11acres)

Woodland Trust

Three Gates Farm reached a significant milestone in the early 1990s when the former market gardening and fruit farm came into the Woodland Trust's care. Today, some of the old fruit trees, mature hedgerows and remnant poplar/alder wind

breaks are still visible, retained as an important link to the past.

The soil is very fertile here so the young oak, ash, field maple and wild cherry trees, planted throughout the 1990s, have become quickly established.

Wide grassy rides make wandering a pleasure and there is a choice of circular routes. This is a haven for rabbits as well, hence a tree guard or two for protection.

Nearby is St Mary's Wood, a small triangular new woodland in the village of Aldeby that was gifted to the Trust in 1995 and planted with native broadleaves by the local community.

MAP 2

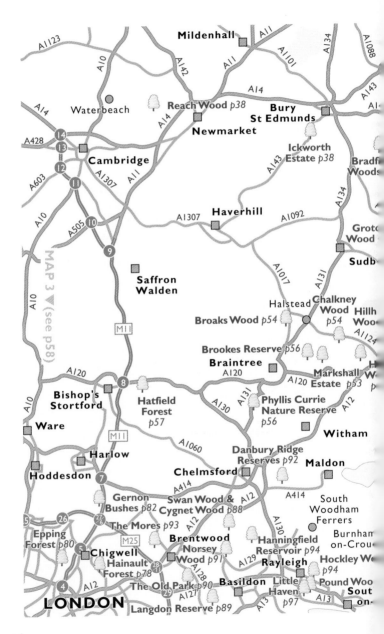

A1123

Mildenhall

A11

A134

A1088

A10

A142

A11

A1101

Waterbeach

A14

Reach Wood *p38*

Bury
St Edmunds

A1

A428

⑭

Newmarket

A14

A143

⑬

Ickworth
Estate *p38*

Bradfi
Woods

Cambridge

A143

A603

⑫

A1307

A11

A134

⑪

A10

A505

⑩

Haverhill

A1307

A1092

Groto
Wood

⑨

Sudb

MAP 3 ▼(see *p58*)

Saffron
Walden

A1017

A131

Halstead Chalkney
Wood Hillh
Woo

A10

Broaks Wood *p54*

A1124

MII

Brookes Reserve *p56*

Braintree

A120

Markshall
Estate *p53*

H
W
p

A120

⑧

Bishop's
Stortford

Hatfield
Forest
p57

A131

A130

Phyllis Currie
Nature Reserve
p56

A2

A10

Ware

MII

Witham

Harlow

A1060

Danbury Ridge
Reserves *p92*

Maldon

Hoddesdon

⑦

Chelmsford

A414

South
Woodham
Ferrers

A414

⑤ ㉖

Gernon
Bushes *p82*

A130

Swan Wood &
Cygnet Wood *p88*

A12

Epping
Forest *p80*

㉗

The Mores *p93*

Burnham
on-Crou

M25

Brentwood

Hanningfield
Reservoir *p94*

Chigwell

Norsey
Wood *p91*

A129

Rayleigh

Hockley Wo
p94

Hainault
Forest *p78*

㉘

A128

④

A12

The Old Park *p90*

Basildon

Little
Haven
p97

Pound Woo
Sout

㉙

A127

A13

on-

LONDON

Langdon Reserve *p89*

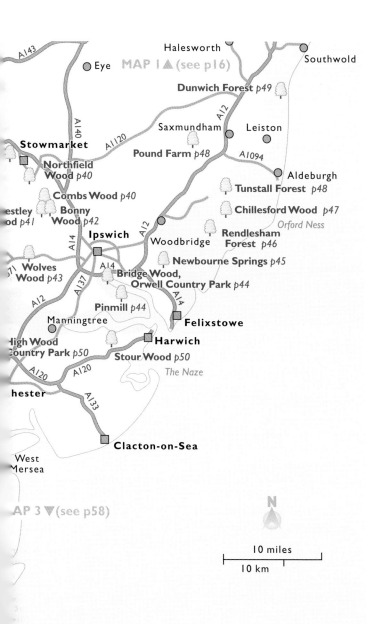

MAP I ▲ (see p16)

Halesworth

Southwold

Eye

Dunwich Forest p49

A143

A140

A1120

Saxmundham

Leiston

Stowmarket

Pound Farm p48

A1094

Northfield
Wood p40

Aldeburgh

Combs Wood p40

Tunstall Forest p48

estley
od p41

Bonny
Wood p42

Chillesford Wood p47

Ipswich

A12

Orford Ness

Woodbridge

Rendlesham
Forest p46

Newbourne Springs p45

A14

Wolves
Wood p43

A137

Bridge Wood,
Orwell Country Park p44

A12

Pinmill p44

Manningtree

High Wood
Country Park p50

Harwich

Felixstowe

Stour Wood p50

The Naze

hester

A120

A133

Clacton-on-Sea

West
Mersea

AP 3 ▼ (see p58)

N

10 miles

10 km

MAP 2

Reach Wood
Reach

Leave A14 at Stow-Cum-Quy exit, following signs for Stow. Continue on B1102 and after Swaffham Bulbeck, take left fork to Reach. (TL565659)

5ha (11acres)

Woodland Trust

Reach Wood was planted in a single day by volunteers from the nearby villages of Reach and Swaffham Prior. The 3,200 young trees on this former arable field forms part of an initiative to create new woodland in England's least wooded county.

Wide, sweeping rides around the site lead to an open meadow that was sown with chalk-loving plant seed and is set against a striking backdrop of steep chalk cliffs.

Beech is dominant here alongside oak, ash, wild cherry, field maple and a variety of colourful shrubs such as hazel, hawthorn, dog rose, wayfaring tree and spindle on path edges.

The wood is linked to the village of Reach via Clunch Pit Lane, named after the type of chalk quarried here, which is used locally as a building material. The circular village walk is fun to explore.

Ickworth Estate
Bury St Edmunds

5km (3 miles) southwest of Bury St Edmunds on west side of A143. (TL825619)

236ha (583acres)

National Trust

Prepare for some awesome sights at Ickworth Estate, including remarkable, huge oaks. One is so large that four adults struggle to link hands around the trunk.

Laid out in 1702, this is Capability Brown-influenced parkland, with woods, deer enclosure, vineyard, summerhouse, canal, lake and church.

Most of the woodland edges the estate, though Albana Wood, an extension of the gardens, feels like an arboretum. Featuring some huge ancient broadleaves and conifers. Look out too for a yew avenue with charming sculptures.

Other woodland belts planted in the 18th century were extended in the 19th century to incorporate Lownde and Dairy woods, both of which are ancient oak woodland.

Great facilities include a living-willow play area, deer hide, adventure playground and all-terrain pushchairs for hire. Good trails are well laid out but the further away from surfaced paths, the muddier it can get.

Bradfield Woods
Bury St Edmunds
A134 south from Bury St Edmunds, turn towards Bradfield St George. (TL935581)
73ha (179acres) SSSI
Suffolk Wildlife Trust

Bradfield Woods, one of the country's finest coppiced ancient woods, stands on a spot that has probably been wooded for 8,000 years.

It's teeming with life – there are more than 370 species of flora including dog's mercury, wild garlic, bluebells, oxlip, herb-paris, primrose, early-purple orchid, wood spurge and betony.

The wood has been coppiced since at least the 13th century and is a great place to learn about traditional woodland management, with a working area near the entrance.

A board at the entrance highlights interesting features of the day, the art sculpture trail being highly recommended.

The tree population includes oak, ash, small-leaved lime, field maple, hazel, alder, crab apple and wild cherry. You might also spot roe, red, fallow and muntjac deer – or visit the fishpond bird hide for kingfisher spotting.

Paths are surfaced but can get muddy, so boots are recommended.

MAP 2

Northfield Wood
Stowmarket

Exit A14 signposted Harleston.
From village take road signposted
to Onehouse. Wood on left
behind houses. (TM023600)
33ha (82acres)
Woodland Trust

Moves to restore Northfield
Wood to its original native
broadleaf cover are paying off.

The wood is starting to open
up, and wide rides re-
established. Beautiful wild
flowers associated with ancient
woodland including oxlip,
ramsons, wood anemone, wood
spurge, herb-paris and orchids
are making a comeback.
Displays in summer are
beautiful, particularly along the
ride edges.

Other parts remain
coniferous, with their
associated 'Christmassy' smells,
where it is not uncommon to
catch sight of deer running
through.

The northeast corner
features two ponds and an old
boundary marked by pollarded
oak and ash trees.

Where the paths tend to
get muddy boardwalks have
been laid.

Combs Wood
Stowmarket

From A1308 take Combs Road via
Combs Ford. At top of hill park
left after church and follow public
footpath onto reserve.
(TM054568)
17ha (41acres) SSSI
Suffolk Wildlife Trust

Wherever you look there are
pointers to the ancient origins
of Combs Wood – in fact the
site was probably originally
primeval forest.

The area is featured in the
Domesday Book – as 'a wood
for 16 swine' and certainly
there is evidence of its origins
on the site, not least the large
perimeter banks.

Interestingly, one ride –
known as Prospect Avenue –
was cut in the 18th century. At
that time the wood was
connected to Combs Hall by a
long-forgotten formal garden.

Carpets of flowers along the
woodland floor are the result
of centuries of coppicing.

Notable are the moscatel and greater butterfly orchid, oxlip and wood anemone. Butterflies such as the orange tip and peacock abound among the nectar-rich plants.

A typical dawn chorus could witness nightingale mixed with chiffchaff, willow warbler, and blackcap.

Priestley Wood
Needham Market

From Needham Market take B1078 towards Barking. Wood south of road just before village, 1.5km (1 mile) from Needham Market. (TM080530)
23ha (57acres) SSSI
Woodland Trust

Considered to be one of the finest woods in Suffolk for its plant life, Priestley is packed with historic and floral importance.

A tour of the wood confirms its classic ancient woodland roots, thanks to such signs as woodbanks and boundary pollards. A wonderfully rich plant population is testimony to the wood's long, uninterrupted tree cover.

You can encounter several species of orchid, nettle-leaved bellflower, wild garlic, broad-leaved helleborine and primrose on a spring/early summer visit.

Centuries of coppicing have produced gigantic, ancient ash and field maple stumps that are still producing healthy growth. Notable among the trees to be found here are the small-leaved lime and hornbeam but the most remarkable, being the rarest of all native trees, is the wild pear – another ancient woodland indicator.

Nightingales add their crystal-clear song amongst the dense coppice and the secretive woodcock may be heard, but less frequently seen, toward dusk.

MAP 2

Bonny Wood
Needham Market

Exit A14 at A140 junction and follow B1078 to Barking from roundabout. (TM076520)
20ha (49acres) SSSI
Suffolk Wildlife Trust

If you're looking for a place to escape, visit Bonny Wood. It may be a bit of a trek to reach this classic old woodland, but being off the beaten track makes it relatively undisturbed.

Records of the wood date back to 1251 and you can sense the history among its oak, ash, field maple and hazel.

Bonny by name and beautiful by nature it's a haven for wildlife, with tawny owls, treecreepers and all three native species of woodpecker. Early risers can enjoy a magnificent dawn chorus from nightingales, willow warblers and blackcaps. Or wait for dusk when there's a good chance of spotting deer or hearing the woodcock's mating call.

Coppicing was reintroduced in 1987 and you can already see the results: wider rides, summer-visiting birds and more varied flowers. Between April and June there's a good display of orchids, herb-paris, anemone, woodruff, ramsons and twayblades.

Groton Wood
Hadleigh

Turn off A1141 to Kersey. Turn left in village past church and head towards Kersey Tye. Straight through Kersey Tye, wood 800m (0.5 mile) on right from village. (TL977428)
21ha (52acres) SSSI
Suffolk Wildlife Trust

Rich in history, this ancient woodland is noted for its coppiced small-leaved lime, an indication that the northern section may have existed since prehistoric times.

The southern part, dating back to the 17th century, features oak, hazel, ash and wild cherry, a favourite of the elusive hawfinch.

There are more than 20 ponds, home to frogs, toads and great-crested newts. Flowers such as violet helleborine, woodruff, herb-paris, bluebell, pignut and early-purple orchid add their colour in spring.

Notable residents include the dormouse, which makes its home in the hazel coppice, and the nightingale – a familiar sound in summer. Other birdlife to look out for are treecreeper, all three woodpecker species, woodcock and nuthatch.

Wolves Wood
Hadleigh

3km (2 miles) east of Hadleigh on northern side of A1071.
(TM055440)
37ha (91acres) SSSI
RSPB

A lovely example of coppiced ancient woodland, this is also one of England's wettest, with no fewer than 46 ponds supporting a variety of aquatic wildlife.

Head to the western part of the wood on a May evening to hear many of the 50 bird species that breed here vocally marking their territory. Why so? Since coppicing was reinstated, conditions have improved for nightingales, blackcaps, whitethroats, garden and willow warblers.

Higher up in the wood you might spot tits, woodpeckers, nuthatches, spotted flycatchers and, if you're particularly lucky, the elusive hawfinch.

A clear and wide circular path is provided but is prone to getting muddy in places. If you enjoy flowers, seek out the ride edges where you'll discover yellow archangel, herb-paris and three types of orchid.

Fine orchid display

MAP 2

Bridge Wood, Orwell Country Park
Ipswich

Exit A14 at Nacton junction and follow A1189 towards Ipswich. After 200m turn left to country park and follow track over A14 bridge turning immediately right to car park. (TM187407)

31ha (77acres)

Ipswich Borough Council

Bridge Wood, in the popular Orwell Country Park, is a cocktail of conifer and broadleaved trees – and a great place to spot foxes and roe deer.

There are beautiful oaks, dating back more than 400 years, and a veteran chestnut tree. You will notice that some trees have been pollarded while others – mainly hazel, elm and sycamore – have been coppiced, producing multiple stems at their base.

Springtime produces a good display of bluebells, wood anemone and moschatel with foxgloves following in summer. Listen out for woodpeckers, nuthatches and nightingales.

It's worth taking a look at the rest of the country park, with a walk by the impressive Orwell Bridge to the heath and scrublands of Pipers Vale.

Pinmill
Ipswich

Take B1456 to Chelmondiston. In village turn left to Pinmill. Car park on left. (TM206378)

26ha (64acres)

National Trust

An unusual route leads visitors into Pinmill Wood. Approached via the River Orwell foreshore, you pass by Thames barges, once important coastal trading vessels. Walking further along you can see boats of a different kind moored along the estuary – many are permanent homes.

At high tide, however, the foreshore path is under water, so an alternative route is necessary. This leads right, out of the car park and 50 metres to steps, at the top of which is a path to the Hoppit House where you enter the wood itself.

Old alder, sycamore, elm, ash, hazel and large oaks await.

Newbourne Springs
Woodbridge

Take A12 north towards Woodbridge, at roundabout turn right to Newbourne. In the village turn left at the church and left again following nature reserve signs. Car park 100m on left. (TM273433) 13ha (32acres) SSSI
Suffolk Wildlife Trust

Newbourne Springs affords a chance to explore a good variety of different habitats within quite a small area.

It takes just 60 to 90 minutes to cover the site, which packs in swamp alder carr, reedbeds and ponds and drier woodland on slopes that lead to open heathland.

Signs of hazel coppicing, new planting, bird boxes, cleared bracken, new hedges, boardwalks and waymarker posts all bear witness to the fact that this is well-cared-for woodland.

The route is fairly easy, thanks to a boardwalk on an easy-to-follow path – though less abled visitors should be aware that some boardwalks are narrow and slippery in the wet and some paths become muddy.

An information centre in an old pumphouse features helpful displays showing habitats, plants and animals on the site – but it's wise to check for opening times.

Hazlenuts

MAP 2

Rendlesham Forest
Woodbridge

From A12 take A1152 round Woodbridge. Turn right onto B1084 towards Orford. Rendlesham Forest Centre is approx 6km (4 miles) along this road on right. (TM353484) 1500ha (3,700acres)

Forestry Commission

Rendlesham Forest is well worth a visit, by foot or cycle and, thanks to an events programme and special play area, it's great for kids.

Hire a bike and tackle one of two off-road family cycle trails or take one of the three circular walks designed for various abilities.

Rendlesham Forest

The woodland is a mixture of conifer and broadleaves with heathland – important for conservation – and wetland. Ironically, the diversity of the wood was enhanced by the Great Storm of 1987 which prompted a redesign of the forest.

While there, take the Phoenix trail through the different forest habitats: conifer plantations of Corsican and native Scots pine – an important timber source; heathland which supports a whole range of birds (including the threatened woodlark and nightjar, the latter being adopted as a symbol for the area) and wetland – an important habitat for amphibians and dragonflies.

Chillesford Wood
Woodbridge

From A12 take A1152 around Woodbridge. Turn right onto B1084. Once through Butley, wood is on left. (TM378518)
61ha (151acres)
Forestry Commission

A wide ride, edged with Scots pine towering above bracken, leads up from the road and blends to Corsican pine as it rises up further.

Being a working plantation, visitors witness the cyclical nature of woodland management from closely grown dark, dense corners ripe for harvesting, to more-open areas with single trees growing tall and proud. A little further along are neat rows of newly planted trees with a pheasant or two scratching about beneath.

It may be predominantly coniferous but twisting hornbeam and lovely sweet chestnuts grow along the woodland edges, providing a tasty autumn treat for those who enjoy roasting chestnuts.

The absence of waymarkers or an information board needn't be an obstacle to enjoying a circular walk, as this can be easily achieved by following the main ride to the top and then turning right, right and right again

After all that exercise, a welcoming lunch can be had at the 15th-century Froize Inn, Chillesford.

MAP 2

Tunstall Forest
Aldeburgh

From A12 take B1078 to Tunstall.
Wood accessed from this road.
(TM380560)
950ha (2,348acres)
Forestry Commission

Autumn is one of the best
times to visit, with maples
providing a stunning display of
vivid yellows and orange.

You could easily spend a day
here, dividing time between the
woodland and the commons –
a good variety of habitats and
wildlife to discover.

Broadleaves line the road and
ride edges, but at its heart are
conifers at various stages of
thinning. Light-filled glades
contrast starkly with blocks of
dense, dramatic shade.

Well-established oak, beech
and sweet chestnut rising above
areas of bracken add their
autumn colour. An open area
of heathland is being managed
to aid conservation.

While waymarkers and route
information aren't easy to
come by, anyone with a
reasonable sense of direction
will find it hard to get lost,
thanks to the grid-like
network of rides.

Pound Farm
Saxmundham

Follow B1119 east of Framlingham
towards Saxmundham. Take third
turning on right to Great
Glemham. Car park on right after
200m. (TM325629)
90ha (222acres)
Woodland Trust

Set in a rolling landscape of
farmland, woodland and
hedgerows, Pound Farm is
making an important

contribution to replenishing East
Anglia's lost heritage.

Arable farmland until the
1990s, it features pockets of
ancient woodland, ponds and
wildflower meadows. Since 1990
more than 60,000 trees have been
planted, resulting in 148 acres of
new native woodland with many
trees more than six metres tall.
The ride edges are peppered with
wild flowers such as lady's
bedstraw, meadow saxifrage, white
campion and betony.

Open and welcoming, the
meadows are attractive in early

summer with their swaying grasses and colourful mix of oxeye daisy, meadow buttercup, bird's foot trefoil, salad burnet, black medick, selfheal and yarrow. A great place for children to play.

An extensive ride network, open spaces, information boards and car parking facilities are provided to bring maximum enjoyment to visitors.

Oak sapling

Dunwich Forest
Southwold

From A12 take B1122 and then left onto B1125. Take northern-most road into Dunwich. Car park on right. (TM461712 & TM468709) 485ha (1,200acres) AONB
Forestry Commission

Visitors tackling the three-mile trail will discover the delights of four contrasting habitats: conifers to broadleaves, heathland to marsh.

Dunwich has a high proportion of fast-growing conifers. Corsican pine was planted in 1969 and there will soon be some majestic examples. Further down the slope is Douglas fir.

In the forest clearing the nationally rare woodlark has made its home, so the area is being maintained to ensure it remains a welcoming habitat.

Broadleaved trees include oak, beech, birch, elm and the wild cherry which, when covered with flowers, makes a spectacular spring sight. In summer the heathland is perfumed with coconut-scented gorse flowers which fill the air. Alder and birch thrive in wet areas, which also provide a rich habitat for toads, frogs, newts, insects and bats.

A Roman road runs through the south of the forest – thought to be one of a network connecting Dunwich with the forts enforcing the Pax Romana.

MAP 2

Stour Wood

Stour Wood
Harwich

From A120 Harwich to Colchester Road turn onto B1352 towards Bradfield. Wood to right of road just before cross roads to Wrabness. Car park off B1352. (TM190310)

54ha (134acres) SSSI

Woodland Trust

Set in the heart of Constable country, Stour is a traditional chestnut coppice woodland dating back to at least 1675.

This is the only place in Essex where woodland leads naturally to saltmarsh – a great place to spot wading birds.

Beside the chestnuts grow oak and the rare wild service tree and beneath, bramble, hazel, birch and aspen thrive.

The coppice management has attracted a wealth of birds and butterflies – no fewer than 40 species of breeding birds including redpoll and wren, and uncommon butterfly species including the white admiral. Dormouse is amongst the 14 species of mammal living here.

High Wood Country Park

Chanterelle car park off A1232 on the Highwoods estate. To reach visitor centre follow signs for A&E hospital or Colchester North railway station and then brown tourist signs. (TL999268)

121ha (300acres)

Colchester Borough Council

Once part of a Royal Hunting Forest, High Wood is just 20 minutes walk from Colchester town centre. Surrounded by housing, retail and commercial development, the country park provides a peaceful wildlife-rich haven and a breath of fresh air for the people of Colchester.

Consisting largely of woodland, parkland and

grassland, the park also boasts a lake fed by a stream running through the central valley. A great place to unwind, picnic, walk, cycle and feel close to nature.

Its Green Flag status is reflected in the quality of experience a visitor might expect. As well as a lively education programme, the park offers volunteer-led walks year-round ranging from ¼ mile to 2 miles every other Friday and Sunday from the visitor centre.

Surfaced paths with gentle inclines means many routes are suitable for wheelchair and pushchair users and there are benches along the way.

Hoe Wood
Marks Tey

From Colchester take A12 towards Chelmsford. At Marks Tey, turn towards Aldham then left into Tey Road by the Big Oak. Wood is 800m (0.5 mile) on right (TL904261)
9ha (22acres)
Woodland Trust

Dating back more than 400 years, Hoe Wood is ancient woodland that was once coppiced to produce a sustainable supply of timber. Today's thriving deer population, with its enthusiasm for eating young shoots, defeated recent attempts to reintroduce this traditional practice.

Large oak trees are a feature, growing amongst wild service, dogwood, sweet chestnut, wild cherry, aspen and holly. In spring the woodland floor comes alive with bluebells, bugle, foxglove, wood avens, primrose, campion, speedwell and violets. Common twayblade and early purple orchids can be seen here and there.

The wood is drained by a network of ditches which feed ponds edged by intriguingly named plants such as water dropwort, figwort, tufted hair-grass, marsh bedstraw and creeping jenny.

A public footpath leads into the wood and, once inside, there is a circular path with good views over the Colne Valley to the north.

MAP 2

Hillhouse Wood

Hillhouse Wood
West Bergholt

From village of West Bergholt, follow signs to the old church of St Marys. (TL945280)

13ha (33acres)

Woodland Trust

A mosaic of different woodland types makes Hillhouse Wood particularly interesting – and well worth the trek along a track from the car park on the edge of the village.

Soon after entering the wood you encounter such delights as a pond, recently opened up and already a magnet for dragonflies and also, as a result of hazel coppicing, a seasonal carpet of bluebells covering the woodland floor in spring.

Summer birdlife includes the nightingale, blackcap, garden warbler, sparrowhawk and hobby. Blackthorn bushes on the ride edge attract the white lesser hairstreak butterfly.

This is a wet, undulating woodland with two ponds and two streams running through but volunteers have been busy creating footbridges and drying out the path edges.

By contrast, nearby Fordham Hall estate, a 500-acre farm donated to the Woodland Trust in 2001, will become the largest new native woodland in the east of England through a major tree-planting programme.

Markshall Estate
Coggeshall
Follow brown tourist signs on A120 north of Coggeshall.
(TL840252)
809ha (2,000acres)
The Thomas Phillips Price Trust

Markshall Estate has all the ingredients of a great day out, the highlight of which is its unique 120-acre arboretum featuring the amazing 700-year-old 'Park Oak'. This woodland giant, with a circumference of eight metres, is the sole surviving pollarded oak from the site's days as a deer park.

The landscaped grounds and park include fine avenues of oak, lime and horse chestnut (at the end of which lives a family of owls), ornamental lakes, the cascades of Robins Brook and the recreation of a 17th-century walled garden.

Beyond the deer park are 500 acres of woodland – home to fallow deer, owls, woodpeckers and sparrowhawks. Mature oak dominates Bungate Wood while Crowlands Wood in spring brings the sight of bluebell carpets and the sound of nightingales.

Visitors should also look out for small-leaved lime trees and plants such as yellow pimpernel, woodruff, early purple orchid and wood-sorrel, butterfly orchid, orpine and herb-paris.

MAP 2

Chalkney Wood
Earls Colne

From A120 take B1024 north towards Earls Colne. Turn right after 3km (2 miles) and left at next T-junction. Lay-by to Essex County Council part of wood on right. To access Forestry Commission section continue along road towards Earls Colne and as road takes sharp bend to left, turn right up track to car park. (TL869282) 73ha (180acres) SSSI

Forestry Commission/Essex County Council

Chalkney has something of a 'dual personality', due in part to its shared ownship.

Spring is a good time to see the stunning display of wood anemones and bluebells, aided by a programme of work which is restoring the native broadleaved woodland and reintroducing coppicing.

Small-leaved lime, hornbeam, sweet chestnut and hazel along with mature oaks, sycamore, elm and ash are all present here. Children could be tasked to find as many different-shaped leaves as possible during their walk.

A first time visitor is advised to enter from the Forestry Commission car park and follow the 1.3 mile waymarked trail interspersed with helpful information boards. As it can get muddy after wet weather be sure to don wellingtons first.

Broaks Wood
Sible Hedingham

Take A131 north from Braintree and then A1017 towards the Hedinghams. Wood on right just before Sible Hedingham sign. (TL784317) 62ha (153acres)

Forestry Commission

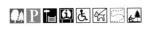

Parents of young children seem to love Broaks Wood. No wonder – it's full of short walks, lots of different woodland types and interesting features such as bird hides and ponds.

The main route is clearly marked and well surfaced, if a little on the muddy side in winter, and you can spend a good hour or more taking everything in – including its

Broaks Wood

history. For Broaks is ancient woodland - known as Ruebroche Wood during the 12th century – and there are lots of telltale signs, including 12th- and 13th-century pottery sites, woodbanks, rare wild service trees and rich flora.

Owned by the Forestry Commission since 1956, it's now a working wood with conservation a priority. At the start of the trail are coppiced sweet chestnut, hazel and ash trees while other sections are quite dense and dark with conifers.

MAP 2

Brookes Reserve
Halstead or Earls Colne

From A120 east of Braintree,
follow signs to Greenstead Green.
Wood 3km (2 miles) north of
Stisted on left. (TL816266)
24ha (59acres) SSSI

Essex Wildlife Trust

Named after 18th-century
owner Thomas Brookes, this
pleasant open grassland site
is surrounded by ancient
coppice woodland.

This wet wood with 12
ponds boasts a good variety of
flora ranging from dog's
mercury to greater butterfly
orchids and sweet woodruff.
Keep an eye open for historic
green lanes that crisscross
the site.

Oak is the dominant large
tree but you'll also come across
small-leaved lime, hornbeam,
ash and hazel and this is a great
place to witness a revival of
coppicing on a grand scale.
Charcoal burning is still
practised in the wood.

There's a sizeable deer
population and nesting birds
include nuthatches,
treecreepers and lesser spotted
woodpeckers. A visit in early
spring will be rewarded with
fine birdsong.

Phyllis Currie Nature Reserve
Great Leighs or Braintree

Entrance in Dumney lane, Great
Leighs. Take road to Felsted from
A131 at St Anne s Castle public
house. Dumney Lane is first right
turning. (TL723182)
4ha (9acres)

Essex Wildlife Trust

Water is a central theme of this
attractive nature reserve which
slopes down to meet a
tributary of the River Ter.

Perhaps the greatest
attraction is a large central lake
created in the 1960s to which
tufted duck, kingfisher and
heron are among its regular
visitors. Fed by a network of
streams and ditches, these
channels together with the
open water are important for
the 13 species of dragonfly and
damselfly that breed here.

Grassland, sheltered glades
and sunny rides support a host

of colourful butterflies –
more than 20 species have
been recorded.

Through careful
management Essex Wildlife
Trust is increasing the wildlife
value of this delightful site,
making it an important piece
of the local countryside.

Hatfield Forest
Bishop's Stortford

Exit M11 at junction 8, take A120
towards Braintree. After 3km
(2 miles) turn right opposite
Green Man public house in Takely
Street, signposted Hatfield Forest.
Car park on right. (TL547208,
TL546199)
228ha (562acres) SSSI
National Trust

A popular haunt with family
visitors, you get a real sense of
history as you explore the well-
laid-out nature trails, walks and
impressive open parkland areas
of Hatfield Forest.

That's not surprising when
you consider this ancient
woodland site is a rare
surviving example of a
medieval royal hunting forest –
it was King Henry I who
introduced fallow deer here
for sport.

The woodland is a cocktail
of different habitats – grassland,
ancient woodland and
marshland – all of them well
managed. And the winding
path, which leads through
each, provides good access for
pushchairs and bikes.

You don't have to venture far
from the car park before it
leads to an open parkland area
where it is difficult not to be
impressed by an array of
enormous pollarded
hornbeams and oaks.
Continue on the winding
path and it will lead you to
a lake, surrounded by heath
and marsh, where fishing
is permitted.

MAP 3

Kempston Wood *p110*
Bedford
Biggleswade
Newport Pagnell
Milton Keynes
Reynold & Holcot Wood *p110*
Rowney Warren *p112*
Royston
Maulden Woods *p112*
Letchworth
Baldock
Hitchin
Leighton Buzzard
Bramingham Wood *p113*
Luton
Stevenage
Dunstable
Aylesbury
Sherrardspark Wood *p86*
Welwyn Garden City
Hertford
Tring Park *p68*
Ashridge *p71*
Tring
Hemel Hempstead
Hatfield
Broxbourne
Wendover Woodland Park *p67*
Wendover
Dancersend Nature Reserve *p66*
Berkhamsted
Bencroft Woods *p83*
Wormley & Nut Woods *p84*
Piggotts Wood *p64*
Hockeridge & Pancake Woods *p65*
St Albans
Danbury Common *p88*
Nor Gre *p87*
Penn Wood *p62*
Amersham
Harrocks Wood *p72*
Berrygrove Woods *p74*
Enfield
Philipshill Wood *p60*
High Wycombe
Kings Wood *p63*
Hodgemoor Wood *p61*
Ruislip Woods *p73*
Watford
Barnet
Fryent Country Park *p75*
Hig Wo
Beaconsfield
Harrow
Marlow
Maidenhead
Gutteridge & Ten Acre Woods *p74*
Hampstead H
Henley-on-Thames
Slough
Uxbridge
LONDO
Windsor
Richmond
Staines
Kingston upon Thames
Woking
Sutton
Epsom

10 miles
10 km

N

58

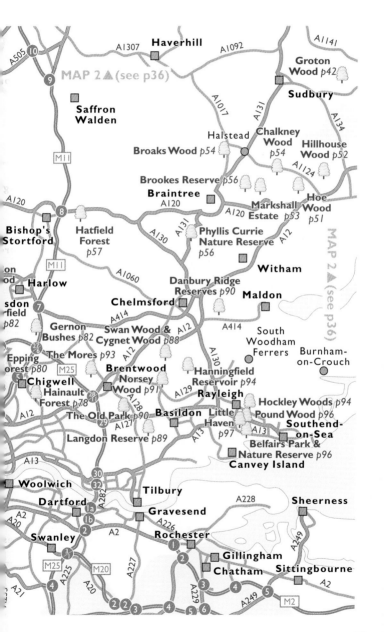

MAP 2 ▲ (see p36)

Haverhill

A1307

A1092

A1141

Groton
Wood p42

Sudbury

A134

A505

10

9

Saffron
Walden

M11

A1017

A131

Halstead

Chalkney
Wood
p54

Hillhouse
Wood p52

Broaks Wood p54

A1124

Brookes Reserve p56

Braintree

A120

Markshall
Estate p53

Hoe
Wood
p51

A120

A120

8

A130

A131

Phyllis Currie
Nature Reserve
p56

A12

Bishop's
Stortford

Hatfield
Forest
p57

MAP 2 ▲ (see p36)

M11

A1060

Witham

on
od

Harlow

Danbury Ridge
Reserves p90

Maldon

sdon
field
p82

7

Chelmsford

A414

A414

South
Woodham
Ferrers

Burnham-
on-Crouch

Gernon
Bushes p82

Swan Wood &
Cygnet Wood p88

A12

A130

The Mores p93

A12

Epping
orest p80

M25

Brentwood
Norsey
Wood p91

Hanningfield
Reservoir p94

Chigwell

Hainault
Forest p78

A12

A128

A129

Rayleigh

Hockley Woods p94

Pound Wood p96

The Old Park p90

Basildon

Little
Haven
p13

Southend-
on-Sea

A127

p97

Langdon Reserve p89

A13

Belfairs Park &
Nature Reserve p96

A13

Canvey Island

Woolwich

30

32

Tilbury

A228

Sheerness

Dartford

1a

A282

Gravesend

A2

1b

A226

A249

A20

2

A2

Rochester

Swanley

3

A225

M25

M20

A227

Gillingham

Sittingbourne

4

A20

Chatham

A2

A21

3

4

M2

2 2 3

4

A229

5

M2

5 6

59

MAP 3

Philipshill Wood
Chorleywood

Turn off A404 at traffic lights toward Chorleywood Station. Pass station on left and under railway line joining Shire Lane. At top of hill road bends sharply to left, but take the turning ahead into Old Shire Lane. Spaces to park in lane after it turns to dirt track.
(TQ010947)
31ha (77acres) AONB
Woodland Trust

Philipshill Wood

A treasure trove of stunning wildflowers typical of ancient woodland sites can be found just minutes from the urban sprawl of London

Philipshill Wood boasts bluebell, wood anemone, wood-sorrel, dog rose, wood mellic and several species of orchid and offers welcome and quiet seclusion for local people who visit the site regularly for walks.

This woodland was cleared and planted with beech and conifers in the late 1960s. Young beech, which was once

produced commercially on this site, now dominates.

A green lane, known as Old Shire Lane, running on the eastern boundary of the wood, is believed to be part of the ancient boundary separating Wessex and Mercia. Other ancient earthworks can be found in the wood plus a boundary stone which is likely to be glacial.

Hodgemoor Wood
Chalfont St Giles

Turn off A355 between Amerston & Beaconsfield opposite Mulberry Bush pub (Bottrells Lane) Car park 1.5km (1 mile) on right. (SU967938)
118ha (292acres) SSSI
Forestry Commission

The Chiltern Heritage Trail runs through this distinctive woodland, whose very name, based on the Saxon 'Hodd', meaning folk of the area, evokes a long and varied history.

Records date Hodgemoor Wood back to the 13th century and the presence of wood banks, venerable pollarded hornbeam, sunken tracks and chalk and flint pits affirm a wealth of uses, underlining its ancient origins.

Walkers can draw year-round access, thanks to a network of footpaths, permissive bridleways and a waymarked trail. These lead to a central ancient woodland core.

Oak and beech dominate but there are also extensive ash and hornbeam stands with groves of cherry and aspen on more fertile and wetter sections. Below these taller trees is a dense shrub layer of thorn, hazel, field maple, birch and holly. Young birch and oak are already emerging following felling of spruce and pine planting.

MAP 3

Penn Wood
Penn Street, Nr. Amersham
South of A404, between High
Wycombe and Amersham.
Reaching Penn Street, park
adjacent to the Common/Cricket
Ground on main street. Take care
not to obstruct access to houses.
(SU914959)
177ha (437acres) AONB
Woodland Trust

Penn Wood

In an area renowned for its rich stock of ancient woodland, Penn Wood, at its very heart, stands out as one of the largest.

The wood forms part of a mosaic of semi-natural ancient woodland and wood pasture, grassland and scrub, rich in wildlife and flora including at least 10 plants not commonly found in the county. It has a good bird population and a number of nationally scarce invertebrates.

Some of its older inhabitants include the remains of an ancient beech and a veteran oak, along with a scattering of trees dating back more than 200 years.

Archaeological features dot the site, among them wood banks, flint and clay pits.

A community group, who successfully fought off attempts to develop a golf course on the site remain as helpful guardians today. Penn Wood is well served with a network of paths.

Kings Wood
High Wycombe

From centre of High Wycombe take A40 east for 3km (2 miles) then turn left into Cock Lane, 2.5km (1.5 miles) to edge of Tylers Green. Kings Wood accessed from lay-by on left just past first house. (SU891941)
75ha (186acres)
Wycombe Parish Council

Well used and treasured by local people, this beech-dominated woodland sits on the crest of a hill overlooking High Wycombe.

The wood has been worked by man for centuries and remains in active management today, a fact sometimes difficult to believe in this tranquil setting with its quiet paths.

Oak, ash and cherry flourish here, along with holly, thorn and a grove of coppiced whitebeam.

Several wood banks, often topped by veteran beech, can be seen – notably along the southern edge. Within the wood the storm of 1987 opened up areas to create new habitats such as glades and wide rides, encouraging a diversity of plants, mammals and birds.

Many features of the wood have evocative names: Chepping ponds, Heartbreak Hill, Yaffle Glade and Brian's Bridge. These can all be seen on a circular walk.

MAP 3

Piggotts Wood
High Wycombe

Take A4128 north of High
Wycombe for 3km (2 miles). Stay
in Hughenden valley, and after
another 1.5km (1 mile) turn left at
the Harrow pub towards Speen.
At North Dean turn right up
narrow and steep track to Piggotts
Hill. Park at top on right in lay-by,
opposite Glasyers. (SU853987)
20ha (49acres) AONB
Dr N Wheeler Robinson

A visit to Piggotts Wood is to
be savoured even before you
arrive, since the journey is a
delight, through valleys
seemingly untouched by time.

The semi-natural ancient
woodland is managed for
recreation and wildlife but
there is evidence of a vibrant
and varied woodland industry,
including the remains of 30
old sawpits, charcoal hearths
and quarries. There are many
old tracks and boundary
banks, lynchets, and at least
two sites with evidence of
early (Iron Age) metalworking.
Over the last decade thinning,
felling and replanting have
added to its diversity.

Most of the beech was first
planted in the 18th century for
the local furniture industry
and statuesque trees give the
margins of the wood an open
feel, providing views across
the valley.

Higher up are young ash,
beech, cherry and oak with a
dense understorey of birch,
holly and hazel. Botanists may
note coralroot bittersweet,
yellow bird's nest orchid,
violet helleborine and green
hellebore. Red kites nest in
the wood.

The farmhouse was the
former home of stonecarver,
wood engraver and
typographer Eric Gill who
died in 1940 – look out for his
crucifix on one of the trees.

Hockeridge & Pancake Woods
Berkhamsted & Chesham

Off A41 at A416 towards
Chesham. Right at Ashley Green
(Hog Lane) then right at T-junction
(Johns Lane) past Johns Lane Farm.
Park on roadside lay-by on right.
(SP978063)

74ha (183acres)

Royal Forestry Society

A varied site, with stands of
hardwood, softwood and
specimen trees – 52 different
species can be found on the
ride edges.

While a lot of replanting was
carried out in the 1950s there
is a mixture of ages and species
– Scots pine, spruce, hemlock
and larch along with beech,
oak and cherry.

The gnarled hornbeams
covering banks and ditches
indicate man's use of the
woods for centuries. Indeed
much of the wood you see
today is on an old Iron Age
field system – it was cleared by
our ancestors and replanted
afterwards. The mix of habitats
provides homes for various
insects and birds.

As minor paths branch off in
all kinds of directions a
compass is recommended.

Hornbeam

65

MAP 3

Dancersend
Nature Reserve
Wendover

On B4009 4km (2.5 miles) northeast of Wendover. Take unclassified road just south of A41/B4009 junction, then right at next T-junction. Drive 1.5km (1 mile) to Thames Waterworks. Car park on left of main waterworks building. Cross road to reserve entrance. (SP905088)
47ha (116acres) AONB, SSSI

Berkshire, Buckinghamshire and Oxfordshire Wildlife Trust

Beguiling by name, Dancersend could be 100 miles away from the bustle of the nearby A41.

The reserve sits in a tranquil valley and its beautiful mosaic of meadow, scrub and woodland creates a mood of calm and contemplation with views down across the valley.

A wide range of plants thrive on the chalk grassland – including rare orchids such as greater butterfly, the Chiltern gentian and meadow clary. The sights and smells of common and fragrant basil, thyme and marjoram feed the senses while also sustaining butterflies and moths including the green hairstreak and day-flying burnet moths.

Much-changed since the 1940s when felling took place, the wood is now managed to conserve survivors of the wildwood such as stinking hellebore and the rare yellow bird's nest orchid. Towards the year's end, look out for scarlet elf cup and earth star fungus.

Owners request dogs are kept on a lead at all times.

Wendover Woodland Park

Wendover

Between Wendover and Tring on
the B4009, take right turn,
north of RAF Halton, signposted
St Leonards and Wendover Wood.
Access 200m on right. (SP887105)
325ha (803acres) AONB

Forestry Commission

You can enjoy several hours
rambling through the woods,
stopping occasionally to enjoy
views across the Aylesbury
valley and the Chilterns.

Recent extensions to the car
park bear testimony to the
popularity of the wood, which
provides a variety of routes to
meet the needs of hundreds of
visitors – from paths and
permissive bridleways to a
fitness trail, cycle tracks and an
orienteering course.

Literally a stone's throw from
the car park you can soak up
stunning views and appreciate
the varied character of the
woods, with its mix of beech,
ash, oak, birch, Norway maple,
spruce, hemlock, larch and
Scots pine.

Many conifers have been
felled to encourage
regeneration of hardwood
trees. The site is also managed
to encourage nesting, breeding
and feeding opportunities for
one of its more unusual
inhabitants, the scarce firecrest,
which lends its name to the
circular trail.

Firecrest

MAP 3

Tring Park

Tring

Just south of A41. (SP927105)
106ha (261acres) AONB, SSSI

Woodland Trust

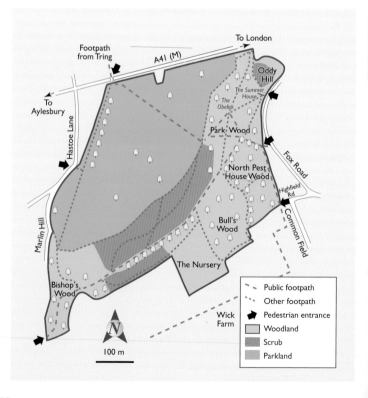

To London

Footpath
from Tring

A41 (M)

Oddy
Hill

To
Aylesbury

The Summer
House

The
Obelisk

Hastoe Lane

Park Wood

Fox Road

North Pest
House Wood

Highfield
Rd

Marlin Hill

Bull's
Wood

Common Field

The Nursery

Bishop's
Wood

Wick
Farm

N

100 m

- – Public footpath
···· Other footpath
➤ Pedestrian entrance
  Woodland
  Scrub
  Parkland

Tring Park

A walk through Tring Park evokes a sense of the rich history of this unusual parkland, which is believed to date back to 1066.

Wealthy banker Lionel de Rothschild bought the estate at auction in 1972 and his son Nathaniel – the first Lord Rothschild – made sweeping changes to the mansion and surrounding farms and cottages. Lord Rothschild opened a zoological museum on the site as a gift to his son Walter, who was responsible for introducing numerous exotic animals to the park. Wallabies, cassowaries, quaggas and rheas used to roam the extensive grassland, which is still grazed today by rather less exotic sheep and cattle.

Consequently, Tring Park is an impressive site to explore and is great for relaxation, particularly in the attractive open areas dotted with large individual trees and the occasional new planting.

The woodland is concentrated on the upper slopes where the mixed broadleaves and conifers include ancient beech, ash and

69

MAP 3

Yellow Rattle

yew with scattered sequoias and elegant yew and lime avenues. At its heart is an obelisk dedicated to Nell Gwynn, and the summerhouse where she is said to have met Charles ll.

A strip of land sandwiched between grassland and woodland is the second largest area of unimproved chalk grassland in the county and one of Hertfordshire's most important habitats with a rich array of butterflies such as skippers and purple emperor, orchids and plants. In summer the grassland is a patchwork of lady's bedstraw, yellow rattle, saxifrage and salad burnet.

King Charles Ride, a long-distance footpath, runs through the site and provides wonderful views across the Chilterns. The Ridgeway National Trail is being redirected along the bridleway at the top of the scarp.

Ashridge
Berkhamsted

Take A4251 towards Tring, turn right at Northchurch onto B45056 to Ashridge. Visitor centre and monument car park on left. (SP971131)
900ha (2,224acres) AONB, SSSI
National Trust

Great views, good for children, and some magnificent-looking trees – just three reasons to visit the Ashridge estate in the Chiltern hills.

Covering six square miles of land between Berkhamsted and Ivinghoe Beacon, it features woods, common land and chalk downland, with good car parking. A number of vantage points offer splendid views across the estate, including Ivinghoe Beacon – a little walk away but well worth it. Steps lead to a large monument, dating back to 1832, which is open April to October at weekends and bank holidays.

Impressive old trees can be found in the open woods, which feature oak, beech and ash. The paths are wide and firm, occasionally surfaced, and provide access from the monument into the surrounding woodland and open commons.

A popular attraction for parents of young children, and dog owners, with a visitor centre open daily April to October.

71

MAP 3

Harrocks Wood
Chandler's Cross

Travelling south on A41 towards
Watford, turn right at traffic lights
in Hunton Bridge. Once in
Chandler s Cross, turn left into
Rousebarn Lane. (TQ066977)
45ha (110acres)

Woodland Trust

Harrocks is linked via a series of
footpaths to four other sites:
Whipendell Wood (managed by
the local authority), Merlin's
Wood, Dell Wood and
Newland's Spring (also managed
by the Woodland Trust). So you
can enjoy five contrasting sites
in just one visit.

When the estate was broken
up and sold off 100 years ago,
the larger mature beech, oak
and ash trees were felled. The
birch and sycamore seen today
are a legacy of the former estate.

Spring brings a fantastic
display of bluebells along with
celandine and primrose and, in
Newland's Spring and Dell
Wood, a carpet of dog's
mercury indicates there's been
a long history of woodland
here. Later in the year you can
see speedwell and campion
along with the more unusual
coralroot bitter-cress.

A programme of coppicing
and opening-up of paths has
resulted in an abundance of
butterflies, including the red
admiral. Muntjac and fallow
deer can be seen too.

Harrocks Wood

Watling Chase Community Forest

The Watling Chase Community Forest sets out to create an attractive landscape where woodland and hedgerows form a mosaic with other land uses. Working in partnership with public and private enterprises, farmers, landowners, voluntary groups, schools, colleges and local people, the aim is to improve the environment for both people and wildlife.

Ruislip Woods
Ruislip

From Ruislip tube station head along the High Street (A4180) to the mini roundabout at the northern end. Fork left, still on the A4180 (Bury Street) before turning right into Reservoir Road. Ruislip Lido is on the right and provides access to Park Wood, Ruislip Common and Copse Wood. Mad Bess Wood can be found by continuing along Bury Street, which becomes Duck s Hill Road. Car park on left up the hill. Bayhurst Wood s car park is off Breakspear Road North.
(TQ086890)
305ha (750acres) SSSI
London Borough of Hillingdon

The Ruislip Woods complex is one of the largest areas of ancient woodland in London, with some parts dating back to the wildwood which covered England after the last Ice Age about 8,000 years ago.

Public outcry saved these valuable woods from development in the 1930s and in 1997 they were designated as the National Nature Reserve in London. The woods are well served by public transport, have good car parks and a horse-riding circuit. The trees are mainly coppiced hornbeam with oak standards.

The site includes a lido, which is a favourite picnic spot, and there is a pub near the main entrance.

MAP 3

Gutteridge & Ten Acre Woods
Uxbridge

Turn off A40 on A437 to Hillingdon. Turn left on Ryefield Avenue and left onto Berkley Road. Park at end of road on Lynhurst Crescent. (TQ086843 / TQ097836)

36ha (89acres)

London Borough of Hillingdon

Big oak trees and a dense understorey, ablaze with bluebells in spring, give Gutteridge a feel of the old wildwood.

Hazel coppice is an attractive feature, along with a great picnic spot in the southeast corner for warm summer days. The surrounding meadows produce colourful displays of wild flowers in the spring, and crackle with the sounds of crickets and grasshoppers. Keep alert for the occasional, electric-blue flash of kingfishers as they dart along the brook.

A narrow, muddy path crosses neighbouring fields to reach Ten Acre Wood. This 100-year-old oak plantation has beautiful hawthorn and blackthorn blossom early in the year that turns to a plentiful supply of berries to nurture birds during autumn and winter.

Berrygrove Woods
Watford, Radlett or Bushey

From Radlett take B462 for 5km (3 miles) to wood entrance by M1 bridge. (TQ134979)

405ha (1,000acres)

Hertfordshire County Council

Part of the 1000-acre Wall Hall Estate, these working woods demonstrate how commercial timber harvesting can be successfully combined with conservation and recreation.

Having crossed fields alongside a golf course to enter the wood, numbered posts then guide your way. Try the 'working woodland' two-mile circular walk from the village of Aldenham.

A section of multi-stemmed coppiced hazel gives way to an area being allowed to naturally regenerate which contrasts starkly with plantations of beech, oak and pine to come. The cherry laurel you see today once provided cover for game birds and, where storms brought down a swathe of mature trees, young ash, beech and cherry are becoming established.

Wide rides encourage wildflowers and butterflies to flourish. Spring brings the reward of carpets of bluebells and wood anemones along the beech ride.

Fryent Country Park
Wembley or Harrow
Fryent Way on A4140.
(TQ196876)
100ha (247acres)
Brent Council

Deep in the heart of London's suburbia lies a wonderful woodland idyll.

Fryent Country Park is a rich mix of organically managed open grassland, hay meadows with more than 500 species of wildflowers that teem with butterflies, fine old hedgerows dotted with imposing mature trees, and 27 ponds. It's a pity Fryent Way – a busy road – bisects the park, but you can escape to Gotfords Hill with its fine panorama across the park and beyond.

Woodland crowns the summit of Barn Hill which provides commanding views over some of London's landmarks. The woodland includes oak, ash, hornbeam, beech, sweet chestnut and elm planted by Humphry Repton in 1783. A 1930s Lombardy poplar avenue produces a distinctive skyline.

Four new woods have been planted since the 1980s – Beane Hill, Lower Hydes, Eastlands and Summers Croft, while a former orchard is being re-established alongside a newly planted cobnut plantation.

MAP 3

Highgate Wood
Camden Town or Highgate

West of B550, Muswell Hill Road.
(TQ280883)
28ha (70acres)
Corporation of London

Once forming part of the Forest of Middlesex and featured in the Domesday Book, the site today remains an important feature of the landscape.

Birdlife ranges from the rare golden oriole to sparrowhawks and there are 180 species of moth and 80 species of spider all recorded here. The impressive list continues with five species of bat as well as intriguing fungi which flourishes in the dead wood amongst oak, hornbeam and the rare wild service tree.

Parts have been fenced off to aid regeneration of the trees and encourage wild flowers such as the bluebell and wood anemone.

There's an excellent visitor centre, jam-packed with information and exhibits, a playground and playing field facilities to keep the children happy, along with a specially designed woodpecker trail. The mile-long history trail is worth a go.

Hampstead Heath
Camden Town and Hampstead

Signposted from A502.
(TQ260865)
320ha (791acres) SSSI
Corporation of London

Hampstead Heath is a people magnet. This vast open space in the very heart of London has everything, from children's playgrounds to a wildlife garden and a very good information centre.

Despite the year-round activity, you can still lose yourself among those huge oak trees where birds such as sparrowhawk, fieldfare, redwing, kestrel, tawny owl and woodpecker make their home. At dusk you could spot one of the many species of bat the wood supports, while some 25 ponds provide habitats for newts, frogs, toads and a multitude of wildfowl.

Hampstead Heath

Children are spoiled for choice with an under fives' centre, traditional playground and paddling pool, interactive displays in the information centre at Parliament Hill Lido and a vast choice of activities, from concerts at Kenwood to sports pitches, and open-air swimming. Not to mention some stunning views of the capital. Exhausting? It's worth it.

MAP 3

Hainault Forest
Chigwell

A112 towards Chigwell Row, continue past sign to Hainault Country Park visitor centre, turn right into Manor Road near church. Car park on right. (TQ475935)

129ha (318acress) SSSI

Woodland Trust

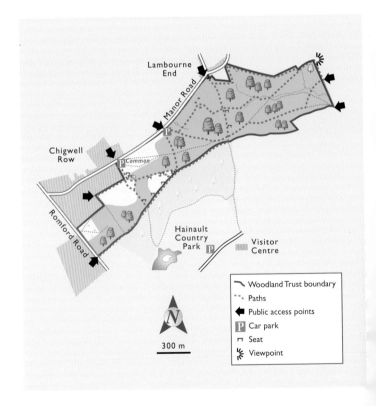

Grand in size, stature and origins, Hainault Forest today is, in fact, just a tiny remnant of what was once the 'Forest of Essex'. Nevertheless this is a site of national historic, cultural and landscape importance.

A former hunting forest created to provide venison for the king's table, it's one of the best surviving medieval forests of its kind, dominated by the distinctive top-heavy, distorted shapes of veteran hornbeam pollards, which the Woodland Trust is working hard to revitalize.

It's estimated that Hainault has around 12,000 such pollards, numerous large oaks and a few ash pollards. The myriad species they support range from owls, woodpeckers and bats to whole communities of specialized insects, lichens, mosses and fungi.

Hainault's status as an ancient woodland is confirmed each spring by its dense carpets of bluebells, which make a stunning display between April and June. The rare wild service tree and butcher's broom (once prized as a scrubbing brush for butchers' blocks) also provide strong evidence of its age.

Another notable feature is a small area of heather heathland – rare in Essex – where key plants such as dwarf gorse and lousewort have been recorded. There is also a pond next to which, it's believed, a local herbalist called Dido lived in the 19th century, producing alternative medicines from the forest's trees and plants.

The forest has contracted steadily over the last 150 years but, with the purchase of 53 hectares (131 acres) of adjoining land, the Woodland Trust aims to breathe new life into Hainault by creating new woodland that will help to buffer and extend the old.

Hainault Forest

MAP 3

Epping Forest
Loughton

Exit M25 at junction 26 or M11 at junction 5 and follow signs.
(TQ412938)
2300ha (5,685acres) SSSI
Corporation of London

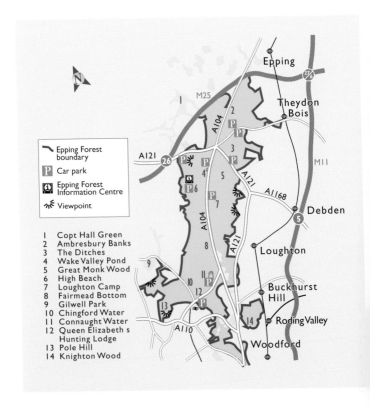

Epping Forest boundary

P Car park

Epping Forest Information Centre

Viewpoint

1 Copt Hall Green
2 Ambresbury Banks
3 The Ditches
4 Wake Valley Pond
5 Great Monk Wood
6 High Beach
7 Loughton Camp
8 Fairmead Bottom
9 Gilwell Park
10 Chingford Water
11 Connaught Water
12 Queen Elizabeth s Hunting Lodge
13 Pole Hill
14 Knighton Wood

Epping Forest

It is possible to spend an entire day in the countryside without leaving London, by exploring Epping Forest. This is the largest public open space in the capital, and two thirds of it is wooded.

Epping Forest dates back thousands of years, although the woods you see today are a 'mere' 1,500 years old. Once a royal hunting ground of the Normans, large parts of the site were earmarked for development in the 19th century. But, in 1878, public concern led to its ownership being transferred to the City of London.

The rich history of Epping Forest is matched by an abundance of wildlife, including all three woodpecker species, nightingales and nuthatches. Scores of ponds and lakes attract waterfowl, great crested grebes and goosander and it's possible to find 650 different plant species including 50 types of trees and shrubs. Oak, birch, beech and lime dominate – some oak trees are spectacularly large and some strangely misshapen – the result of lightning strikes.

It hosts a variety of activities and encompasses the Grade II listed Wanstead Park, two historic listed buildings – Queen Elizabeth's Hunting Lodge and the Temple – and the remains of two large Iron Age earthworks.

The information centre at High Beach houses exhibitions exploring the history of the forest and its inhabitants, has a wide range of books and leaflets and runs a regular programme of guided walks.

MAP 3

Gernon Bushes
Epping

Exit M7 junction 11 and take B1393 towards Epping. Turn left on B181 then first right signposted Coopersale village. Once under railway bridge take immediate left into Gardon Mead. Entrance to wood on left. (TL478030) 32ha (79acres) SSSI
Essex Wildlife Trust

Striking sights here are the amazing hornbeam pollards – beautiful, twisting, gnarled old trees with smooth bark that can take on an eerie air in misty weather.

Much of the wood has an open feel to it, with wide rides cutting between oak and hornbeams.

Ponds, springs which descend down steep-sided valleys, and bogs with patches of rare marsh fern are home to a variety of attractive species including lady fern, bog bean, marsh valerian, kingcup and ragged robin. And don't forget to keep your eyes and ears open for the hawfinch and sparrowhawks which are regular visitors.

This a well-managed site with a surfaced track and boardwalks in muddier sections. Follow the bridleway to the left at the end of Gernon Mead to appreciate the full effect of the pollarded hornbeams.

Thunderfield Grove
Hoddesdon

Take B198 towards Goff's Oak, turn right onto B156 then left onto minor road after 1.5km (1 mile). Take 1st right turn towards Flamstead End and, after 1.5km (1 mile) turn right into Park Lane Paradise. Wood on left after 800m (0.5 mile). (TL338052) 25ha (61acres)
Woodland Trust

Part of the award-winning Broxbourne Woods complex, this former plantation is managed today for the benefit of wildlife and people alike.

At the centre, and a reminder of its commercial forestry days, Corsican pine and western hemlock still dominate. These are being thinned to open up the site and let in more light. Another one-time commercial crop was hornbeam which was coppiced to provide fuel and building timber for London and surrounding areas. Coppicing is being reinstated and trees planted in an attempt to return Thunderfield to its original character.

Paths vary from wide and open to the more secretive and meandering where deer may be spied. The wood supports an abundance of birdlife and is a good place to discover delightful flowers such as dog rose, wood speedwell, bluebell and wood anemone by the brook.

Broxbourne National Nature Reserve is just to the north and well worth a visit.

Broxbourne & Bencroft Woods
Hoddesdon

At roundabout near Hoddesdon Civic Centre follow Cock Lane for 3km (2 miles). (TL327069 & TL326065)
55ha (135acres) SSSI
Hertfordshire County Council

A large deer population has led to some artistic creations in the coppiced parts of Broxbourne and Bencroft Woods where intricate hurdles and basket work deters these animals from grazing.

These woods, together with the Woodland Trust's Wormley and Nut Woods and Hoddesdon Park Wood (see next page) form part of the Broxbourne Woods National Nature Reserve.

The woodland is a mixture of hornbeam coppice, oak, birch, ash, wild cherry and alder and there are also blocks of 1960s conifers, especially in Broxbourne.

Varied and well managed, the woods boast streams, ponds and a wildlife population that includes badgers and grass snakes, woodpeckers, tree creepers, sparrowhawks, woodcocks and buzzards, and butterflies such as orange tip, skipper and speckled wood.

To help visitors access the various trails a map is available locally.

MAP 3

Wormley & Nut Woods
Hoddesdon

From A10, follow Paradise Wildlife Park signs. Continue past Park on White Stubbs Lane and past Bencroft East car park to Bencroft West car park on left. (TL326062) 143ha (353acres) SSSI

Woodland Trust

High on the list of 'must see' woods is this National Nature Reserve with its vast expanse

of ancient woodland populated by huge old oaks that feel centuries old.

Wormley Wood is mentioned in 6th-century documents about Ermine Street, which runs east of the wood. Today it is noted for birds such as hawfinch, redstart and woodpeckers, and its fungi, mosses and ferns, flourishing by pond and stream.

Traditionally coppiced for more than 300 years Wormley had lost around a third of its oak and hornbeam trees to make way for a conifer plantation in the early 1980s. Restoration work is underway, however, with conifers being removed to allow oak, ash, hornbeam and aspen to regenerate. Sweet woodruff, yellow archangel, dog's mercury and bluebell displays welcome in the spring while honeysuckle adds its scent in summer.

The featured seat encircling a tree provides a welcome place to break your walk.

Wormley Wood

Hoddesdon Park Wood

Hoddesdon Park Wood
Hoddesdon

From Hertford town centre take
A414 towards Hertford Heath,
following signs for Balls Park. Minor
road runs south for 5km (3 miles)
to Goose Green. Access wood
from Lord Street on right.
(TL348088)
62ha (154acres) SSSI
Woodland Trust

Hoddesdon Park is a delightful
oak-hornbeam wood with a
decidedly majestic feel. This is
due to the grandness of its
numerous tall, straight mature
oaks and beautiful hornbeam
with their twisted branches
and smooth, grey trunks.

Visit in summer and you'll
be greeted by the heady
scent of honeysuckle which
festoons many of the trees –
a great draw for the white
admiral butterfly.

By following the waymarked
trail you'll get a feel for the
size of the wood as it winds
over a stream and beside an
ancient moat.

Woodbanks fringe three sides
of the wood and are believed to
date back to the Middle Ages.

85

MAP 3

Sherrardspark Wood
Welwyn Garden City

Exit AI(M) at junction 6 and take B1975 to Stanborough. Turn left immediately before railway bridge on Rectory Lane. Car park on right after reservoir buildings. (TL228140)

81ha (200acres) SSSI

Welwyn Hatfield Council

A spacious and undulating woodland with some enormous oaks, Sherrardspark is widely regarded as one of Britain's finest sessile oak and hornbeam woods. Originally called 'Sheregge in Dychenswell' meaning 'bright ridge', it could refer to the white chalk that comes to the surface in the north.

Spring visitors can enjoy a wonderful display of bluebells and anemones as well as rhododendrons along the main ride through May and June.

Access is good, thanks to clearly marked paths and a disused railway line that dissects the western section of the wood and has been resurfaced

Sherrardspark Wood

to form part of the Great North Cycleway. Coppicing has been reintroduced in this part of the wood.

Look out for tame squirrels and the odd muntjac deer or fox. The woodland is also home to all three species of woodpecker, tawny owl, jay, sparrowhawk and hawfinch.

Northaw Great Wood
Cuffley

Exit M25 at junction 24 onto A1000 towards Potters Bar. Turn right onto B157 Shepherds Way and then left on The Ridgeway, signposted Cuffley and Cheshunt. Wood on left. (TL281039) 121ha (300acres) SSSI

Welwyn Hatfield Council

Until 1806, Northaw Great Wood was common land, with coppiced and pollarded hornbeam and sweet chestnut.

Today it's a mixture of oak, birch and areas of ash and sycamore, including two very large, impressive beech trees encountered on one of the three waymarked trails.

Muntjac deer, foxes and badgers plus a varied bird population including nightingales, warblers, woodpeckers, tawny owls, siskin and woodcock sustain interest whatever the time of year. Colour is provided by bluebells, wood anemone, celandine, wood sanicle, ragged robin and bugle.

Paths are provided but it can get muddy so bring boots or wellingtons.

MAP 3

Danbury Common
Danbury

Off A414 from Chelmsford to
Maldon. (TI281044)
86ha (21 acres) SSSI
National Trust

What makes Danbury
Common so interesting is the
large variety of different and
contrasting wildlife habitats
you discover in a relatively
small area.

A waymarked route leads
through most of the different
sections: heathland in the
middle, coppiced woodland
on the edge and northeast of
the site, grassland, and some
young trees.

Away from the few areas of
dense scrub that are virtually
impenetrable, the wood has an
open feel especially where the
blackthorn grows. When
grazing of the commons
stopped in the early 20th
century, scrub took over at
the expense of the heather
and grassland.

It's a good site for families
with a large open area by the
car park that is ideal for picnics
and kite-flying.

Swan Wood & Cygnet Wood
Chelmsford

From Chelmsford take B1007
south towards Billericay. In Stock
turn right into Swan Lane, wood
on right after 400m (0.25 mile).
(TQ688993)
21ha (52acres)
Woodland Trust

Old blends attractively with
new at Swan Wood and its
appropriately named
neighbour, Cygnet Wood.

Swan Wood is an ancient
woodland site, with slopes and
streams, coppicing and
pollarding all adding to its
distinctive character. Internal

Swan Wood

woodbanks, remnants of a medieval boundary and bluebells that burst into delightful colour each May bear testimony that this is indeed ancient.

The wood has been extended all around and on one side the Woodland Trust created a Woods on Your Doorstep site to celebrate the millennium. Cygnet Wood is being left to colonise naturally from Swan Wood.

Other features to look out for are a meadow grazed by horses and a restored old pond.

Langdon Reserve
Basildon

From A127 take B148. At traffic lights turn right signed Horndon-on-the-Hill. Once under railway bridge conservation centre signed on left. (TQ659874)
184ha (458acres)
Essex Wildlife Trust

If you have a fascination for social history, love wildlife or simple enjoy exploring, then Langdon is well worth a day out.

Made up of meadows, woods, ponds, plantations, scrub and former gardens, it offers lots to see complemented by a good events programme.

Worth exploring are the plant-rich Plotlands, including a furnished 1930s Plotland bungalow. These little pieces of countryside were auctioned off in small plots in the early 1900s to people, mainly from the east end of London, after the agricultural depression of the 1890s.

The surrounding scrub and ancient woodland – Lincewood and Marks Hill – are bustling with colour and wildlife, including nightingales and warblers, bluebells and primroses, adders, lizards, butterflies and roses.

Coppicing has been re-introduced at Marks Hill, while the former deer park is 220 acres of hay meadow, where owls start hunting at dusk. Ancient hedgerows, large ponds and an ancient hornbeam wood called Longwood add further variety to your visit.

MAP 3

The Old Park
Brentwood

Take A128 towards Ingrave. After railway crossing turn right, following signs to Thorndon Country Park. After 1.5km (1 mile) turn left to second county council car park. (TQ618906)
55ha (135acres)
Woodland Trust

This is actually a young woodland in an old park.

Well laid-out with meadows, ponds, woodland belts and wide rides, the new design sympathetically links with the past.

The newly planted trees may be little more than 10 years old but this is already a great site to bring children. Combine this with a visit to Thorndon Country Park and you've got a great day out.

Thorndon Park's history, stretching back to medieval times, can be measured in the enormous girth of the ancient trees. Look out for rare English white park cattle and Eriskay ponies which graze here.

The Old Park

Norsey Wood
Billericay

From Billericay take A129 to Wickford. Turn left on Outer Common Road, past church and turn at mini roundabout remaining on Outer Common road. Once over railway line, car park on left. (TQ681951)

67ha (165acres) SSSI

Basildon District Council

Norsey is a great wood for all ages and all abilities, thanks to excellent trails and a fascinating history.

This ancient woodland site has sweet chestnut, oak and hornbeam and has been coppiced for 1,000 years. A working woodyard is open on weekend mornings for the sale of wood products. Coppicing has produced ideal conditions for a ground flora of stitchwort, violet and St John's wort as well as bluebells, wood anemone and patches of lily-of-the-valley. Blackcaps and wrens thrive in these conditions too.

Around the ponds, beside the stream and in glades you'll find such damp-loving tree species as alder, ash and willow and butterflies including brimstone, orange tip and speckled wood.

Thames Chase Community Forest

Thames Chase is one of 12 community forests in England. Its long-term aim is to renew and regenerate the landscape at the edge of East London and South Essex around the towns of Upminster, Romford, Dagenham, Grays and Brentwood. To achieve their target of increased woodland cover from just 8% when it was established in 1990 to 30% by 2030 will require the planting of 5.5 million trees on some 2,000ha (5,000 acres) of land. New woodlands are being created in a wide variety of ways; from small plantings around new development to the greening of mineral extraction and landfill sites and large-scale plantings by the Forestry Commission

MAP 3

Danbury Ridge Reserves

Danbury

A12 east of Chelmsford, take A414 towards Maldon. In Danbury turn left at Eves Corner along Little Baddow Road. After 600m turn right onto Runsell Lane and park on roadside. (TL775064)
101ha (250acres) SSSI

Essex Wildlife Trust

A trail takes you neatly through a mosaic of woodland, common and heathland, streams, bogs and farmland that makes up the reserves.

Dormice live in many parts while the bird population features nuthatch, hawfinch, nightingale and woodpeckers. Brimstone, ringlet and small copper butterflies also thrive here.

Danbury Ridge Reserves

Woodham Walter Common is noted for its sessile oaks with rowan featuring strongly alongside a scattering of wild service trees and alder buckthorn. In spring, Birch Wood is carpeted with wood anemone, wood spurge, wood-sorrel and white climbing fumitory beneath hornbeam coppice.

Lily-of-the-valley is the star turn at Pheasanthouse Wood, a mixed site with three raised bogs, dense sphagnum moss, the rare lesser skullcap and smooth and star sedges. Look out too for oak pollards in Poors Piece, as well as hornbeam and chestnut coppice in Scrubs Wood.

The Mores
Brentwood

A128 from Brentwood. After 3km (2 miles) turn left onto minor road to Bentley. Right after church, wood entrance 300m on left. (TQ565967)
16ha (39acres)
Woodland Trust

This splendid mature woodland set on the urban fringe is an important wildlife refuge, particularly for birds, and features all three species of woodpecker.

Distinctive wet areas, including fine alder woodland, provide unusual habitats. Visitors enjoy access right around the wood thanks to boardwalks provided.

The wood is typical of the area with large, mature oak trees standing high above hornbeam coppice, a reminder that its timber once provided fuel for London. However many oaks, particularly at the western end of the wood, were felled at the end of World War II.

With a good show of spring flowers and a variety of autumn fungi, there is interest at any season.

MAP 3

Hanningfield Reservoir
Billericay

Turn off B1007 into Downham Road and left into Hawkswood Road. The visitor centre entrance is just beyond the causeway opposite Crowsheath Lane. (TQ725972)
41ha (100acres) SSSI
Essex Wildlife Trust

You don't have to be a bird-lover to enjoy Hanningfield Reservoir. Aside from this vast sanctuary for thousands of birds, there are acres of woodland to explore and an excellent visitor centre with fantastic panoramic views.

Known for its waterfowl, there are four hides, one with wheelchair access, which provide vantage points for spotting breeding gadwall, tufted duck and pochard. The reservoir also becomes a feeding ground for 80,000 swifts, swallows and martins each summer.

A third of the woodland to the southeast end of the reservoir – Well Wood and Hawk's Wood – is ancient with remnants of old hornbeam coppice. There are large oak trees with a rich show of bluebells, yellow archangel and stitchwort to enjoy in the spring.

Work is underway to thin out the conifer plantations and open up the rides, glades and ponds.

Hockley Woods
Hockley

From A127 at Rayleigh, take A129 towards Hockley. Continue onto B1013 Hockley Road, entrance sign on right after golf course. (TQ825913)
130ha (321acres) SSSI
Rochford District Council

The largest ancient woodland site in Essex, Hockley Woods is home to the rare heath fritillary butterfly, reintroduced to the site in 1987 – try spotting one in June and July.

Great for youngsters, with a play area close to a large car park, the woodland features a variety of trees – including the rare wild service tree – and signs of an interesting history. Earthbanks in and around the

Hockley Woods

wood hint at its great age.

Some of the wood's large oaks were battered into interesting shapes by the storms of 1987. Also present are sweet chestnut, birch and hornbeam – or look around the ponds, marshes and stream edges for willow and hazel. Wood anemone and wood spurge are followed by cow-wheat's yellow flowers throughout the summer.

There is a wide, surfaced boundary walk but it descends a hill that wheelchair users might find too steep. Parts of the wood get muddy in wet weather so it's a good idea to take wellingtons.

MAP 3

Pound Wood
Thundersley

Turn south off A127 onto A129 and then left onto Daws Heath Road at mini roundabout and bear left, signposted Moorcroft Hall. When road becomes Bramble Road, wood is on left. (TQ816888) 22ha (55acres) SSSI
Essex Wildlife Trust

Home to a variety of wildlife including dormice and badgers, a visit to Pound Wood will be rewarded with a variety of sights and sounds. Parts of the site are dark, with dense undergrowth while other recently coppiced sections are more open.

Essex Wildlife Trust has produced a helpful leaflet describing what you might see. Highlights include the rare wild service tree in the northern part of the wood and an impressive spring bluebell display in the coppice area. Other wild flowers thriving here include the common cow-wheat, yellow archangel, angelica, wood spurge and figwort.

Sweet chestnut and birch can be found on the plateau and ridges of the site, with hornbeam and holly on the slopes and hornbeam, ash, willow, aspen and hazel along the three valley streams.

Look for signs of early medieval woodbanks.

Belfairs Park & Nature Reserve
Southend-On-Sea

From A127 take road to Leigh. Traffic lights at T-junction turn right into Eastwood Road. Look out for old green Belfairs Park sign on left and turn right opposite this on track signposted Riding School for Disabled and Golf Club. (TQ820870 & TQ830870) 73ha (180acres) SSSI

Southend-on-Sea Borough Council

Dissected by a golf course, it can take a little determination to get into Belfairs Park as there is no immediately obvious entrance to the wood.

Populated by some very tame squirrels, the woodland – mainly hornbeam, oak, birch and sweet chestnut – is rimmed by a riding track. A separate nature reserve is fenced off but accessible through a gated entrance. Here the atmosphere is very different, almost secret though well used, with much denser undergrowth, and a delight to explore.

Coppicing and pollarding has been taking place for centuries and the observant will spot woodbanks dotted here and there, hollows from gravel extraction and even small ponds evolved from bomb craters.

A programme of guided walks can be enjoyed from April to October.

Little Haven
South Benfleet

Turn south off A127 at Rayleigh Weir onto Rayleigh Road (A129) and left onto Daws Heath Road at Woodmans pub mini roundabout. Wood on left. (TQ811889) 37ha (92acres)
Essex Wildlife Trust

Welcoming entrance with gates, information board and surfaced route suitable for less able visitors encourages you to explore the mix of woods, scrub, meadows and ancient hedgerows that lie within.

The first of three woods, Starvelarks, may once have been a sweet chestnut plantation. Here the traditional management practice of coppicing is being reintroduced. Then it's over the meadow to Wyburns Wood which feels very different. Ancient woodland with oak, hornbeam, hazel and some sweet chestnut and, in wetter parts, you'll find alder, hazel, male fern, pendulous sedge and honeysuckle.

The meadows are being managed without fertilizers and mown to encourage wildflowers and grasses to establish. A bridge over the stream leads to Tile Wood boasting big, old oak trees and hazel coppice. Here you may glimpse the great spotted woodpecker and common blue butterflies in spring/summer.

MAP 4

Leicester

Oakham

A606

Stamford

A16

Southey Wood *p100*

A15

A47

Oadby

Uppingham

A6003

Bedford Purlieus *p101*

Peterborough

A6

A43

A47

Longueville Wood *p102*

A1

17

16

A15

Market Harborough

A427

Corby

A427

Oundle

A1(M)

Rothwell

A6003

A43

A6116

A605

Sawtry

Aversley Wood *p104*

A508

A14

A508

A43

A510

A509

A45

A6

Kettering

A605

A14

Archer's Wood *p102*

A5199

A428

Wellingborough

Rushden

Hinchingbrooke Country Park *p105*

Brampton Wood *p106* Bram

A6

16

15a

15

Northampton

A428

A509

A6

St Neots

Waresley & Gransden W

A5

A43

A428

A421

A603

Kempston Wood *p110*

Bedford

Biggles

A600

A5508

Newport Pagnell

A421

Milton Keynes

14

M1

Reynold & Holcot Wood *p110*

A6

Row Warr *p112*

A422

A508

A422

A5

13

A507

Maulden Woods *p112*

Letchw

Buckingham

A421

A4146

A5

A4012

12

A5120

Hitchin

A6

A505

Steven

N

Leighton Buzzard

Bramingham Wood *p113*

11

Luten

10 miles

10 km

A505

Dunstable

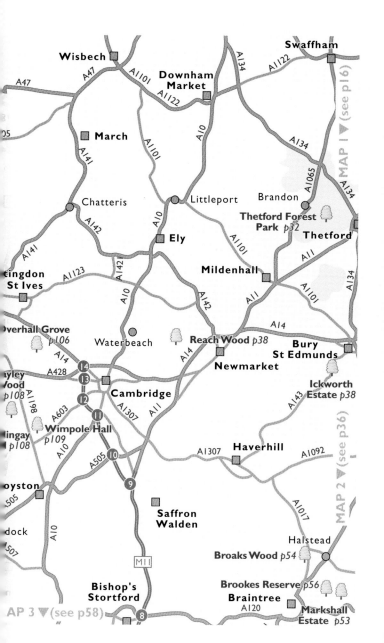

Wisbech

A47

A1101

A47

Downham
Market

A134

A1122

Swaffham

MAP 1 ▶ (see p16)

05

March

A141

A1101

A1122

A10

A1065

Chatteris

A141

A142

A10

Littleport

Brandon

A134

A134

Ely

A101

Thetford Forest
Park p32

Thetford

ingdon
St Ives

A141

A1123

A142

A10

A142

Mildenhall

A11

A1101

A134

verhall Grove
p106

A14

Waterbeach

Reach Wood p38

A14

Bury
St Edmunds

A14

Newmarket

Ickworth
Estate p38

A428

14

A198

A603

13

12

Cambridge

A1307

A11

A143

ayley
ood
p108

11

Wimpole Hall
p109

A10

A1307

Haverhill

A1092

ingay
p108

10

A505

A1017

oyston

505

9

Saffron
Walden

MAP 2 ▼ (see p36)

dock

507

A10

M11

Halstead

Broaks Wood p54

Brookes Reserve p56

AP 3 ▼ (see p58)

Bishop's
Stortford

8

Braintree

A120

Markshall
Estate p53

99

MAP 4

Southey Wood
Peterborough

Located on minor road between villages of Upton and Ufford, 11km (7 miles) west of Peterborough.
(TF110025)
69ha (171acres)
Forestry Commission

A magnificent cathedral-like stand of Corsican pine trees, planted in 1916, greet the visitor at the start of an easy-to-follow trail.

This ancient woodland site was planted with conifers in 1960s so expect to see species such as western hemlock, grand fir and red cedar being thinned and replanted at regular intervals.

Scots pine and beech, oak and ash are also evident, and help sustain a broader range of wildlife. Listen out for the haunting calls of owls and the drumming of woodpeckers. Look deep into the wood for signs of elusive fallow and muntjac deer.

The rides and glades are being opened up to benefit wildflowers and butterflies, adding to the appeal of this pleasant conifer woodland.

If you have time, a visit to Bedford Purlieus (see next entry) provides an illuminating contrast.

Muntjac deer

Bedford Purlieus
Peterborough or Stamford
From A1 take A47 west towards Leicester. After 3km (2 miles) turn left at farm access sign. Keep going until you see Forestry Commission sign. (TL034997)
208ha (514acres) SSSI
Forestry Commission

It's thought that Bedford Purlieus, an ancient woodland remnant of the Royal Forest of Rockingham, sustains a greater variety of plants than any other wood in the country.

In total, some 462 different species of wild flowers, shrubs and trees can be found on this easily navigated site – including the rare large-leaved lime and wild service tree.

The site is made up of a mixture of coppice and high forest – including oak and beech, birch and some conifers – with pockets of limestone grassland.

Thanks to a ride management and scrub clearance programme, the butterfly population is thriving and you might spot white admirals and grizzled skippers among the wild flowers, which include yellow Star-of-Bethlehem and columbine.

Rides are wide, making it easy to walk around but there is no information board or leaflet so visitors must rely on instinct to get around the wood. Public footpaths, however, are signed.

Colourful autumn carpet

MAP 4

Longueville Wood
Peterborough

Follow signs for Orton Longueville
from Peterborough ring road. Past
Notcutts garden centre on left.
Turn right and park on Lady Lodge
Drive. (TL161964)
8ha (20acres)
Woodland Trust

Longueville is an unusual wood
with a real sense of history,
having been planted in the
grounds of Orton Longueville
Hall during the 19th century.

A walk along the wood's
main ride is almost like walking
back through time for the Lord
of the Manor collected exotic
trees while his wife had a
passion for wild flowers.
Wellingtonias planted along the
main avenue have grown
extremely tall, lending a very
grand feel.

The woodland is mixed
conifers and broadleaves –
beech, sycamore, false acacia,
swamp cypress, large oak
pollard and holly. Winter
aconite and snowdrops are the
first flowers to show – followed
by bluebells and wild garlic.

To the east is a large pond
with great crested newts.
Reaching it isn't difficult –
the mainly surfaced track is
wide, providing good access
though sections get muddy in
wet weather.

Archer's Wood
Sawtry

Leave A1(M) at Sawtry exit.
Take turning to Coppingford, at
T-junction turn right. Wood is
800m (0.5 mile) on left.
(TL174810)
18ha (44acres)
Woodland Trust

Parts of Archer's Wood are
believed to be remnants of the
original wildwood, a ditch
and bank in the northern
section is a scheduled ancient
monument and, true to its
name the wood was a
sanctuary for highwaymen.
Even today you can look to
the north and imagine a 14th-
century Cistercian monastic
grange that once stood there.

Flat and easy to access, the
site is dominated by oak, ash
and field maple and served by
a figure-of-eight network of

Archer's Wood

rides so it's great for gentle walks. Be sure to stroll along the main ride to spot the rare and beautiful wild service tree – and look out for foxes, woodpeckers and nuthatches.

Coppicing attracts nesting birds and wild flowers and perhaps the best time to visit is spring when the wood is ablaze with bluebells and alive to the sound of the nightingales.

MAP 4

Aversley Wood

Sawtry

Leave A1(M) at Sawtry exit. After 400m (0.25 mile) turn left into St Judiths Lane, car park is on bend. (TL158815)

62ha (152acres) SSSI

Woodland Trust

A woodland gem in England's least-wooded county, expansive, impressive Aversley Wood is well worth the steep trek (sometimes boggy in winter) required to reach it.

Believed to date back to the Ice Age, it is one of Cambridgeshire's largest ancient woodland sites and a full tour is not for the faint-hearted – but very rewarding, with impressive fenland views.

Wide rides - open and sunny after years of coppicing – make Aversley special: rich in wild flowers, a magnet for butterflies and a haven for birds such as wrens and warblers. You will see plenty of oak and ash and the occasional rare wild service tree while the shrubs lining the rides can be a picture of

Aversley Wood

colourful flowers and berries.

Once part of a 17-mile woodland belt in Saxon times, the wood is also mentioned in the Domesday Book. A medieval boundary bank in the south indicates this section was once open field.

Hinchingbrooke Country Park
Huntingdon

From Huntingdon on A14, take B1514 exit after Swallow Hotel roundabout, signposted Brampton. From here country park is signposted. (TL222718)
73ha (180acres)

Cambridgeshire County Council

The combination of woodland, lakes and open grassland makes for a great place to enjoy a morning or afternoon out with friends and family, particularly children.

A reconstructed Iron Age farm lies close to the lake, very popular during special activity weeks as a venue for craft and farming demonstrations, and there are attractive natural sculptures dotting the landscape.

The woodland is mainly sycamore, ash, oak and beech, some recently planted.

A specially designed mountain bike course, water sports, fishing and camping (by prior arrangement) can all be enjoyed here, as well as walking routes ranging from 30-90 minutes.

MAP 4

Brampton Wood
Brampton

Southbound on A1 take Huntingdon exit. At Brampton Hut roundabout turn right into Brampton, and right again onto Grafham Road. (TL185698) 132ha (326acres) SSSI

Wildlife Trust for Bedfordshire, Cambridgeshire, Northamptonshire and Peterborough

There is a very rural feel to Brampton, Cambridgeshire's second largest wood, which boasts an abundance of flowers, including primroses and bluebells as well as wild pears and no fewer than 29 species of butterfly.

It has hazel coppice, blackthorn and conifers, streams and wide rides, which provide a habitat for 46 different breeding species of bird, including grasshopper warbler, nightingale, spotted flycatcher and woodcock. There are also muntjac and fallow deer here.

Historically the wood was coppiced but this declined and the largest trees were felled during World War II since when it has developed quite a wild feel. However, the Wildlife Trust has reintroduced coppicing since acquiring the site in 1992.

Popular with dog walkers, most of the site sits on chalky boulder clay – and can therefore get muddy – but there are some flat sections and well-drained valleys.

Overhall Grove
Cambridge or Knapwell

From A14 take road signposted to Boxworth. Once through Boxworth turn left at crossroads to Knapwell. On edge of village turn left down a track to the church. Park beneath the trees in front of church. (TL337633) 17ha (42acres) SSSI

Wildlife Trust for Bedfordshire, Cambridgeshire, Northamptonshire and Peterborough

Believed to be England's largest surviving elm wood it also has some of the biggest oaks in Cambridgeshire. Overhall Grove teems with wildlife – bats, owls, insects and fungi all thriving in deadwood habitats.

Featuring one of the largest and oldest known badger setts, a viewing platform allows visitors to observe without disturbing the animals.

It's easy to get a feel for the past in this wood. A moated mound, Overhall Manor, once stood in the northern part, surrounded by field and pasture. Occupied in the 11th century, it was in decay by 1283 but the manor fishponds can still be seen today as mounds and hollows between the wood and nearby church.

A programme of coppicing has been reinstated alongside the paths which provide routes through both northern and southern sections of the wood.

Waresley & Gransden Woods
Gamlingay

From St Neots take B1046 towards Great Gransden. At edge of village take small road on right running southwest towards Waresley. 1.5km (1 mile) down this road is Waresley Dean Bridge; park on grass verge and walk up track. (TL263548)

54ha (134acres) SSSI

Wildlife Trust for Bedfordshire, Cambridgeshire, Northamptonshire and Peterborough

These are excellent woods for escaping to – lovely and peaceful with a real feeling of intimacy, thanks to its relatively narrow paths.

A stream running through a small valley between the two woods adds interest and you can follow its route on the waymarked trail.

Dating back to the Domesday Book, the woodland has coppiced hazel and big ash and oak trees, where oxlip and bluebells add their colour in spring.

A large section of Gransden Wood was felled in 1929 and has subsequently been replanted with beech, hornbeam, cherry and sycamore. The northern section is private.

Seats are provided along the trail which can be muddy – so ensure you wear your boots.

MAP 4

Gamlingay Wood
Gamlingay

From A428 take B1040 to Waresley. Continue towards Gamlingay and wood is just before the town on left. (TL242535)

48ha (119acres) SSSI

Wildlife Trust for Bedfordshire, Cambridgeshire, Northamptonshire and Peterborough

Gamlingay Wood

Gamlingay provides a good mix of conifer and ancient woodland. Home to oak, ash and the rare wild service tree, its woodland floor becomes a riot of flowers, notably bluebell and oxlip, each spring.

Records date back to the 13th century but there is evidence of a greater age in the double ring ditch – probably Iron Age – and medieval woodbanks. Gamlingay witnessed the first British studies in woodland ecology in 1912.

The Wildlife Trust, owners since 1991, has been thinning conifers, recoppicing ash, hazel, field maple and oaks and managing a sizeable deer population.

Bear in mind that, apart from a distinctive central dry section with oaks, birch and bracken, the wood stands on Gault clay so wellingtons are a must in wet weather to make the most of a 60–90 minute exploration of the site.

Hayley Wood
Gamlingay

From A1198 take B1046 towards Great Gransden. Before reaching the village look for a water tower on right and take track opposite up to wood. (TL294534)

48ha (119acres) SSSI

Wildlife Trust for Bedfordshire, Cambridgeshire, Northamptonshire and Peterborough

To see Hayley Wood at its best, visit in spring when bluebells and one of the largest populations of oxlips in the UK are in bloom. At this time of year listen for the nightingale's song too.

Species are thriving in this ancient woodland, thanks to a policy of coppicing reintroduced by the Wildlife Trust in 1962, and a visit helps gain a picture of how traditionally managed woods would once have looked.

Hayley Wood dates back at least 1,000 years and is enclosed by the original woodbank. Ironically, the first wood you encounter is actually secondary woodland – oak, hawthorn, birch and sallow with quite a different 'feel' to the rest of the site, which is classic coppice wood – field maple, ash and hazel coppice set beneath big oak trees.

The wood is served by a waymarked trail but this needs seeking out.

Wimpole Hall
Royston

Exit M11 at junction 12 and follow signs to Wimpole on A603. After 10km (6 miles) turn right, following brown National Trust signs.
(TL336510)
91ha (225acres)
National Trust

Immediately behind the 18th-century house are formal walled gardens and beyond these the landscaped park with a folly, lakes, striking avenues, magnificent parkland trees and woodland belts on higher ground. Charles Bridgeman,

Capability Brown and Humphry Repton all played their part in landscaping the grounds you see today.

Sadly, the once-impressive two and a half mile avenue of elm trees leading to the house was hit by Dutch Elm Disease some years ago but has since been replaced with young lime trees.

If you're feeling energetic, try the walk from Cambridge along the Wimpole Way which brings you through the woodland edge and into the parkland.

It's a great day out for the family, especially if you combine your visit with the working farm as well.

MAP 4

Reynold & Holcot Wood
Cranfield

Leave M1 at junction 13 and follow A421 to Bedford. Turn off A421 just after passing through the village of Brogborough onto a minor road signposted to the Brogborough picnic site. Park at picnic site owned by Bedfordshire County Council. (SP955400)
98ha (242acres)
Woodland Trust

Set on a ridge, this prominent landscape feature offers great views over Marston Vale. Forming part of Marston Vale Community Forest, the site combines the semi-natural ancient woodland of Holcot Wood with a programme of tree planting, pond and meadow creation at Reynold Wood.

Marbled white butterflies can be seen on the new open grassy rides, and look out too for muntjac and Chinese water deer, foxes and hares.

Old hazel and ash coppice are common but you'll also find oak, field maple, Midland hawthorn and hazel. Early spring displays include early-purple orchid, wood anemone, wood sanicle, yellow archangel, primroses and bluebells. And the sizeable bird population includes all three British woodpecker species.

There is a good network of bridleways and paths.

Kempston Wood
Kempston

On A421 take Kempston turn, then left at first roundabout and left again at second, toward Wooton. Straight ahead at crossroads, past pub on right and follow road towards Kempston west end for 800m (0.5 mile). (SP995470)
17ha (41acres)
Woodland Trust

A little off the beaten track, Kempston is a peaceful wood with delightful views across the Marston Vale – a thoughtfully positioned seat helps you enjoy the panorama.

This is a historically important ancient woodland site, with ditch and bank separating an area formerly managed by coppicing from the other where animals were allowed to graze beneath the trees.

Ash, oak and field maple trees, complemented by shrubs such as hazel, blackthorn, spindle, and geulder rose provide a home to woodpecker, nuthatch and tree creeper. There's a good chance of spotting the small muntjac deer during your visit. Spring brings a good show of flowers – among them bluebell, early purple orchid, wood anemone and wood-sorrel.

The paths are generally good, though some sections are rather steep.

Marston Vale Community Forest

Centred on the 'Brickfields', an area of existing and former clay pits stretching 10 miles between the M1 and the southern fringe of Bedford, the Forest of Marston Vale covers over 160 sq km (61 sq miles) in the heart of Bedfordshire. The aim is to recreate the mosaic of woodland, farmland and open spaces that once covered the area, improving access for people and reintroducing traditional management to encourage wildlife and help sustain the rural economy. Patches of ancient woodland, some dating to the end of the Roman occupation, are supplemented by new woodland to create a multi purpose forest that contributes towards the national timber supply, creates attractive sites for public enjoyment, enhances the natural beauty of the countryside and establishes wildlife habitats. The forest offers a growing number of beautiful woodlands, wetlands and open spaces for everyone to enjoy.

WOODLAND
TRUST

Trees and forests are crucial to life on our planet. They generate oxygen, play host to a spectacular variety of wildlife and provide us with raw materials and shelter. They offer us tranquillity, inspire us and refresh our souls.

Founded in 1972, the Woodland Trust is now the UK's leading woodland conservation charity. By acquiring sites and campaigning for woodland it aims to conserve, restore and re-establish native woodland to its former glory. The Trust now owns and cares for over 1,100 woods throughout the UK.

The Woodland Trust wants to see:
no further loss of ancient woodland
the variety of woodland wildlife restored and improved
an increase in new native woodland
an increase in people's understanding and enjoyment of woodland

The Woodland Trust has in excess of 170,000 members who share this vision. For every new member, the Trust can care for approximately half an acre of native woodland. For details of how to join the Woodland Trust please either ring FREEPHONE 0800 026 9650 or visit the website at www.woodland-trust.org.uk.

If you have enjoyed the woods in this book please consider leaving a legacy to the Woodland Trust. Legacies of all sizes play an invaluable role in helping the Trust to create new woodland and secure precious ancient woodland threatened by development and destruction. For further information please either call 01476 581129 or visit our dedicated website at www.legacies.org.uk

Wormley Wood

Further Information

Public transport

Each entry gives a brief description of location, nearest town and grid reference. Traveline provides impartial journey planning information about all public transport services either by ringing 0870 608 2608 (calls charged at national rates) or visit www.traveline.org.uk. For information about the Sustrans National Cycle Network either ring 0117 929 0888 or visit www.sustrans.org.uk

Useful contacts

Forestry Commission, 0845 367 3787, www.forestry.gov.uk
National Trust, 0870 458 4000, www.nationaltrust.org.uk
Wildlife Trusts, 0870 036 7711, www.wildlifetrusts.org
RSPB, 01767 680551, www.rspb.org.uk
Royal Forestry Society, 01442 822028, www.rfs.org.uk
Tree Council, 020 7407 9992, www.treecouncil.org.uk
National Forest, 01283 551211, www.nationalforest.org
Woodland Trust, 01476 581111, www.woodland-trust.org.uk

Recommend a Wood

You can play a part in helping us complete this series. We are inviting readers to nominate a wood or woods they think should be included. We are interested in any woodland with public access in the UK.

To recommend a wood please photocopy this page and provide as much of the following information as possible:

About the wood

Name of wood: _____

Nearest town: _____

Approximate size: _____ ha/acres

Owner/manager: _____

A few words on why you think it should be included:

_____

_____

About you

Your name: _____

Your postal address: _____

_____

_____ Post code: _____

If you are a member of the Woodland Trust please provide your membership number.

Please send to: Exploring Woodland Guides, The Woodland Trust, Autumn Park, Dysart Road, Grantham, Lincolnshire NG31 6LL, by fax on 01476 590808 or e-mail woodlandguides@woodland-trust.org.uk

Thank you for your help

Other Guides in the Series

Chilterns to the
Welsh Borders

The South West
of England

The South East
of England

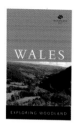

Wales

The Peak District
& Central England

The North East
& Yorkshire

The North West
& The Lakes

Coming soon
Scotland

If you would like to be notified when certain titles are due for publication please either write to Exploring Woodland Guides, The Woodland Trust, Autumn Park, Dysart Road, Grantham, Lincolnshire NG31 6LL or e-mail woodlandguides@woodland-trust.org.uk

Index